University of London
Institute of Latin American Studies Monographs

5

Directory of
Libraries and Special Collections on
Latin America and the West Indies

University of London
Institute of Latin American Studies Monographs

1. The 'Detached Recollections' of General D. F. O'Leary, edited by R. A. Humphreys. 1969.

2. Accounts of Nineteenth-Century South America: an Annotated Checklist of Works by British and United States Observers, by Bernard Naylor. 1969.

3. Commercial Relations between British Overseas Territories and South America, 1806–1914. An Introductory Essay, by T. W. Keeble. 1970.

4. British Nitrates and Chilean Politics, 1886–1896: Balmaceda and North, by Harold Blakemore. 1974.

5. Directory of Libraries and Special Collections on Latin America and the West Indies, by Bernard Naylor, Laurence Hallewell and Colin Steele. 1975.

Directory of Libraries and Special Collections on Latin America and the West Indies

by

BERNARD NAYLOR
formerly Librarian,
Institute of Latin American Studies

LAURENCE HALLEWELL
University of Essex Library

and

COLIN STEELE
Bodleian Library Oxford

UNIVERSITY OF LONDON
Published for the
Institute of Latin American Studies
THE ATHLONE PRESS
1975

Published by
THE ATHLONE PRESS
UNIVERSITY OF LONDON
at 4 *Gower Street, London* WC1
Distributed by Tiptree Book Services Ltd
Tiptree, Essex

U.S.A. and Canada
Humanities Press Inc
New Jersey

0 485 17705 6

Printed in Great Britain by
WESTERN PRINTING SERVICES LIMITED
BRISTOL

CONTENTS

FOREWORD

The Committee on Latin America, which initiated this *Directory*, was established in 1963. It brings together, in the preparation of bibliographical aids for scholars and other interested persons, librarians who have a special concern with Latin America. Its list of *Latin American Economic and Social Serials* was published in 1969, its *Latin American History with Politics: a serials list*, in 1973, and a further list of periodicals in the fields of language and literature is nearing completion.

The three editors of the Directory are members also of the Latin American sub-committee, established in 1972, of the Standing Conference of National and University Libraries. The sub-committee, which is actively exploring ways of improving the provision and exploitation of Latin American materials in the libraries of the United Kingdom, readily supported the proposal to compile a guide to, or a directory of, these collections; and the Institute of Latin American Studies, which is the home of the Union Catalogue of Latin American Library Materials, is happy to publish the completed work.

The *Directory* is complementary, though on a smaller scale, to the *Guide to Manuscript Sources for the History of Latin America and the Caribbean in the British Isles* published by the Institute in collaboration with the Clarendon Press in 1973. The library collections of the United Kingdom are diverse and rapidly expanding. The purpose of this *Directory* is to make them better known and to facilitate their use.

R.A. HUMPHREYS
Institute of Latin American Studies

INTRODUCTION

The Committee on Latin America, of which we three are all members, asked us to compile this directory as a further item in its series of bibliographical publications. We began by circulating a questionnaire to more than 200 libraries throughout the British Isles during the summer of 1972. At the beginning of 1973, we made a second approach to some libraries which had not responded to the first one, and extended our questionnaire's circulation so as to reach more than 300 libraries. The contents of the main section of this book are based on their replies. In addition to recording changes in information which became known to us between the circulation of the questionnaires and the date the copy went to press, we supplied each library with a draft copy of the entry concerning it during July 1973 and invited corrections. The information the directory contains may therefore be considered to be broadly correct up to that date.

Scope
The questionnaire made it clear that Latin America was being interpreted to include the whole of the mainland south of the Río Grande together with the reasonably adjacent islands, though it invited libraries to state whether their own collections related to the whole area or were limited, for example, to the countries of the former British Empire. Individual entries normally make clear the coverage of each library. With the recent publication of the *Guide to Manuscript Sources for the History of Latin America and the Caribbean in the British Isles* (London, Oxford University Press in collaboration with the Institute of Latin American Studies, University of London, 1973), manuscripts could safely be excluded from the directory, which therefore concentrates on printed materials with occasional mention of other types of resources such as discs, tapes, slides, and postage stamps.

Arrangement of the entries
The entries are arranged in alphabetical order of the postal towns in which the libraries are situated, and within each town alphabetically according to each library's own title, or according to the title of the parent organisation. A similar arrangement is used for libraries in the London postal area.

Preliminary information
Each entry begins with essential preliminary information concerning the library described. Postal codes have been supplied and telephone numbers cited according to preferred Post Office form, available STD codes being given in parentheses except for those libraries in towns where all-figure telephone numbers are now the rule. Telex and 'answerback' codes have been provided. Wherever possible, the name of a member of staff with specialist knowledge or responsibility in this field has been provided in addition to that of the chief librarian.

Description and organisation of the collection
The discursive passage which follows the preliminary information attempts to indicate the usefulness of each library to students of Latin America by describing briefly the history of the collection and by indicating special subject or area interests, or strength in particular types of materials. Figures of holdings are quoted whenever possible, but these can frequently be regarded only as general approximations, and it must be added that it is often the strongest libraries which find it most difficult to make a numerical assessment of their holdings. The records of each library's holdings, its author, title and subject catalogues, whether separate or combined, are briefly mentioned, as are the classification scheme each library uses (LC for Library of Congress, and UDC for Universal Decimal Classification are two abbreviations used) and whether the arrangement of the library permits the readers immediate access to the shelves.

Details of services
Further information follows about the services provided by each library.
Hours of opening are indicated. Failing specific information

to the contrary, it can be assumed that libraries are closed on Saturdays and Sundays, and open on bank holidays. Attention must also be drawn to the fact that both Scotland and Northern Ireland have different bank holidays from England and Wales.

Admission briefly states the procedure laid down by each library for the submission of a request for use of its facilities from someone not a member, nor automatically entitled to membership through his relationship with the library's parent body. If a library is not described as 'Open to general public', it can be assumed that a request from such a potential user ought to be reinforced by a statement, either verbal or in writing, of the special reasons underlying the request. Requirements such as a fee or a financial deposit are also mentioned whenever possible.

Enquiries explains how each library is prepared to handle queries, and for which category of users. Though not specifically asked in the questionnaire, some libraries emphasised their readiness to accept queries through Telex, and this has been indicated. It can be assumed that in those other cases where the availability of Telex is mentioned in the preliminary information without being referred to under *Enquiries*, it is also usually available as a method of approach.

Microreading lists the forms of photographically reduced text for the reading of which the library possesses the necessary equipment.

Copying mentions the facilities available for the copying of materials. Readers ought to be prepared to encounter restrictions on the copying of fragile materials, to be required to pay for the provision of photocopies, and in some cases to have to sign an undertaking to respect copyright provisions. The term 'Xerox' is used to cover all types of same-size dry-copy reproduction, not just those produced by Rank-Xerox equipment.

Typewriters. If there are facilities for the use of typewriters, this is also mentioned. Readers ought to assume they must provide their own machine unless the contrary is indicated. Some libraries specifically asked us to point out that typewriters could be used only in a special room set aside for the purpose. We have done as they requested, but should like to emphasise that readers ought not to expect to use typewriters in any library without prior consultation of the supervisory staff, and that it is normal practice in those libraries which permit typewriters to limit their use to a special room.

NOTE. In the case of all the foregoing facilities, each library will clearly be limited by availability of staff, technical aids or space, in the number of calls on its services it can answer, and readers must be prepared to make due allowance for this.

Lending. The broad outlines of each library's lending services are indicated. But in addition to placing limits on the number of items borrowed at any one time, and on the period of loan, each library will have certain categories of material of which it restricts or forbids the loan, for example, periodicals, copyright material, reference works, or heavily used items. These are likely to be the subject of detailed prescription and to vary from time to time, and users are best advised to investigate such restrictions further when they wish to exercise borrowing rights.

Union Record mentions those joint records of the holdings of several libraries, whether published or unpublished, in which the particular library's holdings are recorded. The list of abbreviations explains those used in this section.

Publications. In listing publications, we have limited ourselves principally to publications of or about the library, and especially those which facilitate the reader's use of the collections. Serial publications of some of the parent institutions are also listed in the appendix. We have not attempted to list all their relevant monograph publications.

Appendix

In an appendix, we have recorded further useful information for those working in the Latin American field, the addresses of embassies, national tourist offices, airlines and banks, of 'Anglo' societies where these exist, of interested academic societies, and relevant serial publications.

A combined subject and library title index completes the volume.

As always with volumes of this kind, a great deal is owed to librarian colleagues in the libraries mentioned in its pages and to those not mentioned here who expedited the project with prompt 'nil' replies to our questionnaire. Nonetheless, we must take the blame for any errors. We hope our readers will not be slow to point them out to us, as also to draw our attention (by writing to the Librarian of the University of London Institute of Latin American Studies) to any omissions or to interesting collections we have failed to include. Such is often the most desirable outcome of a volume of this kind. Our thanks are also due to Gloria Jones and Marion Swiny, who helped with the preparation and circulation of questionnaires and the drafting of entries, and to Brigid Harrington who also helped to type and standardise the entries at a later stage. We must also thank our colleagues on the Committee on Latin America, and on the Latin American subcommittee of the Standing Conference of National and University Libraries for their persistent interest and helpful suggestions. We much appreciate the generous attitude shown by our respective employing institutions to the demands the project has made upon our time and professional energies. We are grateful to the University of London Institute of Latin American Studies which, by undertaking the publication of this volume, places us firmly in its debt, and (we believe) markedly increases the debt of gratitude which the other publications it has supported have earned it from scholars.

BERNARD NAYLOR
(University of London)

LAURENCE HALLEWELL
(University of Essex Library)

COLIN STEELE
(Bodleian Library, Oxford)

August 1973

ABBREVIATIONS

(Some of the abbreviations most frequently employed are explained in the introduction)

AIINFS	Associate of the Institute of Information Science
ALA	Associate of the Library Association
ALAA	Associate of the Library Association of Australia
BLLD	British Library Lending Division (see no. 8)
BUCOP	*British union catalogue of periodicals*, 4 vols, London, Butterworth, 1955–8. *Supplement to 1960*, 1962. *New periodical titles 1960–1968*, 1970. *New periodical titles*, 1960– (quarterly with annual cumulations)
BUCLA	British union catalogue of Latin Americana (see no. 81)
COLAESS	Committee on Latin America, *Latin American economic and social serials*, London, published on behalf of COLA by Clive Bingley, 1969
EMRLS	East Midlands Regional Library System, Reference Library, Bishop Street, Leicester. *Tel:* Leicester 20644 extn 15 (STD code 0533). *Telex:* 34643 EM LEICESTER
FLA	Fellow of the Library Association
LASER	London and South Eastern Library Region, 9–10 Alfred Place, London WCIE 7EB. *Tel:* 01–636 9383, 01–636 4684, 01–636 9537. *Telex:* 25616 LASER LONDON
NRLS	Northern Regional Library System, Central Library, Newcastle upon Tyne NE99 1MC. *Tel:* Newcastle upon Tyne 610691 (STD code 0632). *Telex:* via 53373 LIBRARY NTYNE
NWRLS	North Western Regional Library System, Central Library, Manchester M2 5PD. *Tel:* 061–236 7401. *Telex:* 667149 INFORMATION MCR
SCL	Scottish Central Library, Lawnmarket, Edin-

burgh EH1 2PJ. *Tel:* 031–225 5321. *Telex:* 72279
SCOTCENLIB EDIN

SCONUL Standing Conference of National and University
Libraries, c/o The Library, School of Oriental and
African Studies, Malet Street, London WC1E
7HP. *Tel:* 01–637 2388 extn 307

SWRLS South Western Regional Library System, Central
Library, College Green, Bristol BS1 5TL. *Tel:*
Bristol 23962 (STD code 0272). *Telex:* via 44200
CITYLIB BRISTOL

WLSP World list of scientific periodicals, 4th edn, 3
vols, London, Butterworth, 1963–5

WMRLS West Midlands Regional Library System, Central
Libraries, Paradise, Birmingham B3 3HQ. *Tel:*
021–235 2613. *Telex:* 338316 WMRLB BHAM

WRLS Welsh Regional Library System; Aberystwyth
Bureau, National Library of Wales, Aberystwyth.
Tel: Aberystwyth 3816 (STD code 0970). *Telex:*
35165 LLYFRFA ABRWYTH. Cardiff Bureau, Central Library, Cardiff. *Tel:* Cardiff 22116 (STD
code 0222)

LIST OF LIBRARIES

1. ABERDEEN   University of Aberdeen Library
2. ABERYSTWYTH   College of Librarianship Wales Library
3. ABERYSTWYTH   National Library of Wales
4. ASHFORD   Wye College Library
5. BELFAST   Queen's University of Belfast Library
6. BIRMINGHAM   Birmingham Public Libraries
7. BIRMINGHAM   University of Birmingham Library
8. BOSTON SPA   British Library, Lending Division
9. BRACKNELL   Meteorological Office Library
10. BRIGHTON   Brighton Public Library
11. BRIGHTON   Institute of Development Studies Library
12. BRISTOL   University of Bristol. Wills Memorial Library
13. CAMBERLEY   Staff College Library
14. CAMBRIDGE   Cambridge University Library
15. CAMBRIDGE   Centre of Latin American Studies Library
16. CAMBRIDGE   Faculty of Archaeology and Anthropology. Haddon Library
17. CAMBRIDGE   Faculty of Economics and Politics. Marshall Library
18. CAMBRIDGE   Faculty of Modern and Medieval Languages Library
19. CAMBRIDGE   Institute of Criminology. Radzinowicz Library
20. CAMBRIDGE   Scientific Periodicals Library
21. CAMBRIDGE   Scott Polar Research Institute Library
22. CANTERBURY   University of Kent at Canterbury Library
23. COLCHESTER   University of Essex Library
24. COVENTRY   University of Warwick Library
25. DUNDEE   University of Dundee Library
26. EDINBURGH   National Library of Scotland
27. EDINBURGH   Royal Scottish Geographical Society Library

28. EDINBURGH	Royal Society of Edinburgh Library
29. EDINBURGH	University of Edinburgh Library
30. EGHAM	Royal Holloway College Library
31. EXETER	Devon County Library
32. EXETER	University of Exeter Library
33. GLASGOW	Glasgow Corporation Public Libraries
34. GLASGOW	Institute of Latin-American Studies Library
35. GLASGOW	University of Glasgow Library
36. GLASGOW	University of Strathclyde. Andersonian Library
37. GUILDFORD	University of Surrey Library
38. HARPENDEN	Rothamsted Experimental Station Library
39. KINGSTON UPON HULL	University of Hull. Brynmor Jones Library
40. LEEDS	University of Leeds. Brotherton Library
41. LEICESTER	Leicestershire County Library
42. LEICESTER	University of Leicester Library
43. LIVERPOOL	Liverpool City Libraries
44. LIVERPOOL	University of Liverpool Library
45. LONDON	Anglo-Chilean Society Library
46. LONDON	Bank of England Reference Library
47. LONDON	Bedford College Library
48. LONDON	Board of Inland Revenue Library
49. LONDON	Brazilian Embassy Library
50. LONDON	British Broadcasting Corporation Music Library
51. LONDON	British Council English-Teaching Information Centre and CILT Language Teaching Library
52. LONDON	British Film Institute. National Film Archive
53. LONDON	British Institute of Recorded Sound Library
54. LONDON	British Library, Newspaper Library
55. LONDON	British Library, Reference Division. British Museum Library
56. LONDON	British Library, Reference Division. Science Reference Library

57. LONDON	British Museum (Natural History) Library
58. LONDON	British Numismatic Society Library
59. LONDON	Catholic Central Library
60. LONDON	Chartered Institute of Transport Library
61. LONDON	Chartered Insurance Institute Library
62. LONDON	Church Missionary Society Library
63. LONDON	Commonwealth Institute Library
64. LONDON	Commonwealth Secretariat Library
65. LONDON	Corporation of London City Business Library
66. LONDON	Department of Trade and Industry Central Library
67. LONDON	Department of Trade and Industry. Statistics and Market Intelligence Library
68. LONDON	Ealing Technical College Library
69. LONDON	Folklore Society Library
70. LONDON	Foreign and Commonwealth Office. Library and Records Department
71. LONDON	Heythrop College Library
72. LONDON	Hispanic and Luso-Brazilian Council. Canning House Library
73. LONDON	House of Commons Library
74. LONDON	House of Lords Library
75. LONDON	Institute of Advanced Legal Studies Library
76. LONDON	Institute of Archaeology Library
77. LONDON	Institute of Commonwealth Studies Library
78. LONDON	Institute of Contemporary History and Wiener Library
79. LONDON	Institute of Education. Comparative Education Library
80. LONDON	Institute of Historical Research Library
81. LONDON	Institute of Latin American Studies Library
82. LONDON	International Book Information Services Research Department

83.	LONDON	International Coffee Organization Library
84.	LONDON	International Cooperative Alliance Library
85.	LONDON	King's College London Library
86.	LONDON	Lloyds Bank International Limited. Economics Department Library
87.	LONDON	London Borough of Hackney Library Services
88.	LONDON	London Borough of Tower Hamlets Libraries
89.	LONDON	London Library
90.	LONDON	London School of Economics and Political Science. British Library of Political and Economic Science
91.	LONDON	London School of Hygiene and Tropical Medicine
92.	LONDON	Ministry of Defence (Central and Army) Library
93.	LONDON	Ministry of Defence Naval Historical Library
94.	LONDON	National Maritime Museum Library
95.	LONDON	Overseas Development Institute Library
96.	LONDON	Queen Mary College Library
97.	LONDON	Reuters Limited
98.	LONDON	Royal Anthropological Institute of Great Britain and Ireland Library
99.	LONDON	Royal Commonwealth Society Library
100.	LONDON	Royal Geographical Society Library
101.	LONDON	Royal Institute of British Architects. Sir Banister Fletcher Library
102.	LONDON	Royal Institute of International Affairs Library
103.	LONDON	Royal Society of Medicine Library
104.	LONDON	School of Oriental and African Studies Library
105.	LONDON	Trades Union Congress Library
106.	LONDON	Tropical Products Institute Library
107.	LONDON	United Nations Information Centre

DESCRIPTIONS OF LIBRARIES AND SPECIAL COLLECTIONS

ABERDEEN

1 *University of Aberdeen Library*

King's College, Aberdeen, Scotland. AB9 2UB
Tel: Aberdeen 40241 (STD code 0224)
University Librarian: J. M. Smethurst BA, ALA

The library has a small collection on Latin America and the Caribbean, including 7 periodical titles. Special attention is paid to the acquisition of West Indian literature.

Author, title and classified subject catalogues. Dewey classification. Open access.

Hrs: Mon–Fri 0900–2300 (Summer vacation –1700. Other vacations –2200). Sat 0900–1700 (vacations –1300). Sun 1400–1700. Closed 1 and 2 Jan, 25 and 26 Dec, last week of June.

Admission: At librarian's discretion (written application; deposit required).

Enquiries: By post and telephone.

Microreading: Microcard, microfiche and microfilm.

Copying: Microfilm and Xerox.

Lending: To members and through inter-library loan.

Union Record: BLLD, BUCOP.

PUBLICATIONS:

Library handbook.

A. P. Thornton, 'The G. R. G. Conway manuscript collection in the library of the University of Aberdeen', *Hisp. Amer. Hist. Rev.* 36 (3) 1956, pp. 345–7.

ABERYSTWYTH

2 *College of Librarianship, Wales/Coleg Llyfrgellwyr Cymru*

Llanbadarn Fawr, Aberystwyth, Cardiganshire, Wales. SY23 3AS
Tel: Aberystwyth 3842 extn 58 (STD code 0970)

Telex: 35391 CLW ABERYSTWYTH
Librarian: D. Ball FLA

The College library has been collecting material on Latin American libraries and librarianship since 1964, and is especially strong in English language materials.

Author, title, alphabetical subject and classified subject catalogues. Dewey and (for library science) Classification Research Group classifications. Open access.

Hrs: Mon–Fri 0900–2200 (vacations –1730). Sat 1000–1630 (term only). Closed bank holidays except Spring.
Admission: Open to general public.
Enquiries: By post and telephone.
Microreading: Microcard, microfiche and microfilm.
Copying: Xerox.
Typewriters: Permitted.
Lending: To users, and through inter-library loan.
Union Record: WRLS.
PUBLICATIONS:
Guide to the library.
Library link (accessions list).
Current contents (title pages).
Serial publications in European languages (translated contents lists).
Periodicals list.
Annual reports list.
Occasional papers.

3 National Library of Wales

Aberystwyth, Cardiganshire, Wales. SY23 3BU
Tel: Aberystwyth 3816/7 (STD code 0970)
Telex: 35165 LLYFRFA ABRWYTH
Librarian: D. Jenkins MA

The Library has no special collection of Latin American material although the Copyright Act of 1911 has enabled it to acquire a statutory copy of all British publications, including those of Latin American interest. The collection of material on the genealogy, demography and history of the Welsh and Celtic peoples, including the Welsh colony in Patagonia, is emphasised.

Author catalogue. LC classification. Predominantly closed access.

Hrs: Mon–Fri 0930–1800. Sat 0930–1700. Closed Good Fri–Easter Tue, 24–6 Dec.

Admission: Bona fide researchers (prior written application).

Enquiries: By post, telephone and Telex.

Microreading: Microfiche and microfilm.

Copying: Microfilm, Xerox and photostat.

Typewriters: Permitted (with special permission).

Lending: Through inter-library loan.

Union Record: BUCOP.

PUBLICATIONS:

The National Library of Wales: a brief summary of its history and activities, 1967.

Bibliotheca Celtica: a register of publications relating to Wales and the Celtic peoples and languages (annual publication).

National Library of Wales Journal (bi-annually).

ASHFORD

4   *Wye College Library, University of London*

Wye, Ashford, Kent. TN25 5AH

Tel: Wye 812401 extn 242 (STD code 0233)

Librarian: G. P. Lilley MA, FLA

The college has been a school of the University of London in the Faculty of Science (Agriculture and Horticulture) since 1900. The recent establishment of a lectureship in Latin American rural sociology jointly at the college and the University of London Institute of Latin American Studies has been accompanied by a development in the college's library holdings in the fields of agricultural economics and rural sociology, for which special funds have been allocated. The collection is a small one, but is being expanded by purchase through commercial and non-book-trade sources, and by exchange arrangements with organisations in the Commonwealth and the United States.

Author, title and classified subject catalogues. UDC classification. Open access.

Hrs: Mon–Fri 0900–2200 (vacations –1900). Sat 0930–1700

(vacations –1200) Sun 1400–1700. Closed bank holidays, one week at Easter, one week in Summer vacation, and one week at Christmas.
Admission: At librarian's discretion.
Enquiries: By post and telephone.
Microreading: Microfilm.
Copying: Xerox.
Lending: To members and through inter-library loan.
Union Record: BLLD, BUCOP, BUCLA, Kent union list of periodicals.
PUBLICATIONS:
Library guide.

BELFAST

5   Queen's University of Belfast Library

University Road, Belfast, Northern Ireland. BT7 1LS
Tel: Belfast 45133 extn 249 (STD code 0232)
Telex: 74487 QUEENS BELFAST
University Librarian: H. J. Heaney MA, FLA
The library began collecting in the field during the 1960s, but the collection is still very small. Of especial interest are the holdings of legal material, some of which were acquired from the Board of Trade in 1970. Of this material only the Bahamas collection is still being augmented. Some exchanges of legal periodicals with Venezuela and Peru are also a continuing feature.
    Author and classified subject catalogues. LC classification. Open access.
Hrs: Mon–Fri 0900–2300 (vacations –1730). Sat 0900–1230. Closed Northern Irish bank holidays.
Admission: Open to general public.
Enquiries: By post and telephone.
Microreading: Microcard, microfiche and microfilm.
Copying: Microfilm and Xerox.
Lending: To members and (with special permission) non-members, and through inter-library loan.
PUBLICATIONS:
Notes for readers.
Guide to the law library.

BIRMINGHAM

6 Birmingham Public Libraries

Central Libraries
Paradise, Birmingham B3 3HQ
Tel: 021–235 4511
Telex: 33455 LIBRARY BHAM
City Librarian: W. A. Taylor MC, FLA

The Reference Library has 1,300 books and 5 periodical titles on Latin America and the Caribbean which form part of the general collection. The Shakespeare Library collects editions, translations and works of criticism from all sources including Latin America.

Author and classified subject catalogues. Dewey classification. Open access and stack service.

Hrs: Mon–Fri 0900–2100. Sat 0900–1700.
Admission: Open to general public.
Enquiries: By post, telephone, Telex and personal visit.
Microreading: Microcard, microfiche and microfilm.
Copying: Microfilm and Xerox.
Typewriters: Permitted (separate study carrels).
Lending: Through inter-library loan to libraries only.
Union Record: BUCOP, WMRLS, COLAESS.

PUBLICATIONS:

A Shakespeare bibliography: the catalogue of the Birmingham Library, London, Mansell, 1971.

Reprints and various guides to services and departments.

7 University of Birmingham Library

P.O. Box 363, Edgbaston, Birmingham B15 2TT
Tel: 021–472 1301 extn 171
Telex: 338160 UNIVLIB BHAM
University Librarian: K. W. Humphreys BLITT, MA, PHD, HONLITTD, FLA

Only a small proportion of the library's holdings relate to Latin America and the Caribbean, but some emphasis has been given to collecting imaginative literature.

Author and classified subject catalogues. LC classification. Open access.

Hrs: Mon–Fri 0900–2100 (vacations –1700), Sat 0900–1230. Closed for one week at Christmas, one week at Easter, first week of Summer vacation, Late Summer bank holiday and two days following.

Admission: At librarian's discretion (written application).

Enquiries: By post and telephone.

Microreading: Microcard, microfiche and microfilm.

Copying: Microfilm and Xerox.

Lending: To members of the University and through inter-library loan.

Union Record: BUCOP, WMRLS, COLAESS.

PUBLICATIONS:

Introduction to the library.

The University Library regulations.

BOSTON SPA

8 *British Library, Lending Division (National Central Library and National Lending Library)*

Boston Spa, Wetherby, Yorks. LS23 7BQ
Tel: Boston Spa 843434 (STD code 0937)
Telex: 557381 NATLENLIB BSPA
Director General: M. B. Line MA, FLA, AIINFS

Founded in 1959, the *National Lending Library* was established to provide a rapid inter-library loan service for scientific materials, and especially for photocopies of articles from scientific periodicals, the basis for the service being its own very extensive collections of periodicals cited in the standard abstracting and indexing tools. Since 1967, the library has been collecting periodicals in the social sciences, and since 1972 in the humanities, so that it now holds well in excess of 40,000 current titles. In the Latin American field, it is the library's policy to acquire all periodicals cited in the abstracting and indexing tools used by specialists in the field, and to provide a photocopy service on the lines already indicated. Access to the service is through local academic, public and special libraries, which hold stocks of prepaid order coupons, and have adequate resources of reference works to permit accurate description of the material required.

Following the decision to create the British Library (see also nos. 54–6), almost the entire work of the *National Central Library* was transferred to Boston Spa in the summer of 1973. The National Central Library was founded in 1916. It has developed the nation's union catalogues (now housed at Boston Spa) to a point where they contain about four million entries, and are growing at the rate of 250,000 titles, and 500,000 locations a year. But in recent years, it has been the National Central Library's policy to increase the emphasis given to loans from its own stock, which has been substantially improved, especially by the use of selective types of blanket order, for example of the publications of many United States presses. The library's own book stocks, also now at Boston Spa, amount to 750,000 volumes and are increasing at the rate of 70,000 volumes a year.

Enquiries: By post and telephone.
Microreading: Microcard, microfiche and microfilm.
Copying: Microfilm and Xerox.
Lending: Through inter-library loan.
PUBLICATIONS:
Current serials received by the NLL.

BRACKNELL

9   *Meteorological Office Library*

London Road, Bracknell, Berks. RG12 2SZ
Tel: Bracknell 20242 extn 2250 (STD code 0344)
Telex: 848160 WEATHER BKNL; 847010 WEATHER BKNL
Librarian: F. A. Seammen

The library has been collecting in the field since the late nineteenth century, and its collection of over 100,000 volumes includes material on the meteorology (including climatology) and certain aspects of the oceanography and hydrology of Latin America and the West Indies. Holdings include very considerable collections of daily weather reports. Much of the data is acquired as a result of exchange agreements.

Author and classified subject catalogues, supplemented by a climatological catalogue classified by countries. UDC classification. Open access.

Hrs: Mon–Thurs 0830–1700. Fri 0830–1630. Closed bank holidays.
Admission: Bona fide enquirers (prior application).
Enquiries: By post and telephone.
Microreading: Microcard, microfiche and microfilm.
Copying: Xerox.
Lending: To members, and (exceptionally) non-members, and through inter-library loan.
Union Record: BLLD, BUCOP.

BRIGHTON

10   *Brighton Public Library*

Church Street, Brighton, Sussex. BN1 1UE
Tel: Brighton 63005/6 (STD code 0273)
Telex: 87167 INFORM BRIGHTON
Borough Librarian: J. N. Allen, BA, FLA

Although the Latin American holdings number only 363 volumes, acquisition began in 1873, and they include such rarities as B. Hall, *Extracts from a journal written on the coasts of Chili, Peru and Mexico* (1825), W. G. Ouseley, *Description of views in South America* (1852) and C. Waterton, *Wanderings in South America* (1828). 128 of the volumes are in the closed access reference library, the remaining 235 are in the open access lending library.

Author and classified subject catalogues. Dewey classification.
Hrs: Mon 1100–1900, Tues–Fri 1000–1900. Sat 1000–1600. Closed bank holidays.
Admission: Open to general public.
Enquiries: By post and telephone.
Copying: Microfilm and Xerox.
Typewriters: Permitted only in exceptional cases.

Lending: To members and through inter-library loan.
Union Record: BLLD, LASER.

11 *Institute of Development Studies Library, University of Sussex*

Andrew Cohen Building, Falmer, Brighton, Sussex. BNI 9RE
Tel: Brighton 66261 (STD code 0273)
Librarian: M. H. Rogers MA, ALA

The library has been collecting material on the region since 1966 and now has just over 5,000 books and pamphlets and 500 periodical titles. It is a U.N. and UNESCO depository library and concentrates on acquiring national and regional development plans, official statistics, banking journals and reports, and land reform agency publications. Practically no material published before 1960 is collected, although the library has an extensive collection on microfiche of national development plans. Exchanges are undertaken with 75 bodies, such as universities and government agencies, in Latin America.

Author and alphabetical subject catalogues. Unclassified. Partially open access.

Hrs: Mon–Fri 0900–1815. Closed one week at Christmas and one week at Easter.
Admission: At librarian's discretion (written application).
Enquiries: By post and (to members only) by telephone.
Microreading: Microcard, microfiche.
Copying: Xerox.
Lending: To members and (at librarian's discretion) non-members, and through inter-library loan.
PUBLICATIONS:
Holdings list of non-official serial publications.
Guide to information on developing countries in U.S. government publications, 1962–1971.
Rural migration in less developed countries: a preliminary bibliography.
West German, Swiss and Austrian sources of information on Third World countries.

BRISTOL

12 *University of Bristol*

Wills Memorial Library
Queens Road, Bristol BS8 1RJ
Tel: Bristol 24161 (STD code 0272)
Telex: 449174 UNIVLIB BRISTOL
University Librarian: N. Higham MA, ALA

The library contains 1,850 books and 11 periodicals on the region, with particular emphasis on Mexico and Cuba.

Author and classified subject catalogues. LC classification. Open access.

Hrs: Mon–Fri 0845–2130 (Summer vacation –1715. Other vacations –1900). Sat 0845–1300.

Admission: At librarian's discretion (written application, or, for members of other universities, letter of introduction or union card).

Enquiries: By post and telephone.

Microreading: Microcard, microfiche and microfilm (for members only).

Copying: Microfilm and Xerox.

Lending: To members and through inter-library loan.

Union Record: BLLD, BUCLA, SWRLS, COLAESS.

PUBLICATIONS:
Reader's guide.

CAMBERLEY

13 *Staff College Library, Ministry of Defence (Army)*

Camberley, Surrey. GU15 4NP
Tel: Camberley 63344 extn 618 (STD code 0276)
Librarian: K. M. White ALA

The library has been collecting on Latin America and the Caribbean since 1945 and now has 300 books and 5 periodicals. It specialises in acquiring current publications on military and political affairs, with an emphasis on those concerned with insurrection and urban guerrilla warfare. It receives some publications by exchange from the defence ministries of foreign countries.

Author, title and classified subject catalogues. UDC classification (modified). Open access.

Hrs: 0800–2200 (including Sat and Sun).
Admission: At librarian's discretion.
Enquiries: By post and telephone.
Copying: Xerox.
Typewriters: Permitted.
Lending: To members and Ministry of Defence departments.
PUBLICATIONS: (neither available outside Ministry of Defence):
Library bulletin.
Staff College index of periodical articles (quarterly).

CAMBRIDGE

14   *Cambridge University Library*

West Road, Cambridge CB3 9DR
Tel: Cambridge 61441 (STD code 0223)
Telex: 81395 UNIVLIB CAMB
University Librarian: E. B. Ceadel MA

The Library has enjoyed the privilege of copyright deposit since the Act of Queen Anne in 1709 (and before that benefited from the Licensing Acts during the periods 1662–79 and 1685–95), and, since it is a library from which books can be borrowed, it has one of the largest lending collections in England of material in English on Latin America. Although deposit was only partially effective before about 1812, it now embraces not only Irish publications (nominally since 1801) but also (from about the early 1960s), an increasing amount of material from North American publishers which maintain branch offices in London. Regular extensive buying from Latin America started in 1966 (when the university became a Parry Centre) with a total capital grant of £10,000. Annual expenditure since then has been between £2,000 and £4,000 of which at least half has gone on non-current material. Earlier acquisitions of Latin American interest included the library of Lord Acton, which has various materials on the region, books from the library of F. A. Kirkpatrick which was strong on the River Plate countries, and the Conway collection. Conway was a businessman long resident in Mexico, and his library includes many microfilmed documents from the Archivo General de la Nación, particularly documents relating to the treatment by the Inquisition of Jews and captured Elizabethan seamen. Cambridge University Library also possesses some microfilms of United States National Archives holdings relating to Latin America, and has made extensive purchases of nineteenth-century official publications. There is also an extensive map collection.

Author catalogue. Own classification. Open access.

Hrs: Mon–Fri 0900–2200 (vacations –1900). Sat 0900–1300. Closed Good Fri, Easter Mon, 16–23 Sep, 25 Dec.

Admission: Bona fide researchers.

Enquiries: By post and telephone.

Microreading: Microcard, microfiche and microfilm.

Copying: Microfilm and Xerox.

Typewriters: Permitted.

Lending: To members (except 1st and 2nd year undergraduates) and through inter-library loan.

Union Record: BLLD (partly), BUCOP, BUCLA, COLAESS, Cambridge University *Current serials.*

PUBLICATIONS:

Information for new readers.

Readers' guide.

Libraries Information Bulletin.

Current serials.

Classified list of current serials, 1971.

Subject guide to class 'Ref', 1968.

J. Street, 'The G. R. G. Conway collection in Cambridge University Library: a checklist', *Hisp. Amer. Hist. Rev.* 37 (1) 1957, pp. 60–81.

15 *Centre of Latin-American Studies Library, University of Cambridge*

History Faculty Building, West Road, Cambridge CB3 9DR

Tel: Cambridge 61661 (STD code 0223)

The library has a small reference collection (400 books, 22 current periodicals) for the use of graduates, which is looked after on a part-time basis by the secretary of the Director of the Centre.

Author and geographical subject catalogues. No classification. Open access.

Hrs: Mon–Fri 0900–1700.
Admission: Graduate researchers.
Lending: None.
CENTRE PUBLICATIONS:
Working papers.

16   *Faculty of Archaeology and Anthropology, University of Cambridge*

Haddon Library
Downing Street, Cambridge CB2 3DZ
Tel: Cambridge 59714 extn 24 (STD code 0223)
Librarian: Mrs J. Green BSC

The library which was established in 1884 has been collecting Latin American material within its main field of interest, and particularly that relating to Amerindians, since 1904. Present Latin American holdings (excluding pamphlets) are 600 books and 25 periodical titles, additions to the collection being predominantly of current material.

Author and alphabetical subject catalogues. Own classification. Open access.

Hrs: Mon–Fri 0900–1730 (vacations 0915–1700). Sat 0900–
1700 (term only). Closed one week at Easter, 3 weeks in late Aug/early Sept, and one week at Christmas.
Admission: At librarian's discretion (application in writing or by telephone preferred).
Enquiries: By post and telephone.
Copying: Microfilm and Xerox.
Lending: To members and through inter-library loan.
Union Record: BUCOP, Cambridge University *Current serials.*

17 *Faculty of Economics and Politics, University of Cambridge*

Marshall Library of Economics
Sidgwick Avenue, Cambridge CB3 9DB
Tel: Cambridge 58944 (STD code 0223)
Librarian: Miss M. Hannigan

The library dates from 1925. Latin American holdings are 100 books, 40 pamphlets and 40 periodical titles, out of a total stock of some 55,000 items.

Author and classified subject catalogues. Own classification. Open access.

Hrs: Mon–Fri 0900–2200 (vacations 0900–1300, 1415–1700). Sat 0900–1900 (vacations –1300). Closed 7 days at Easter, Spring bank holiday, 7 days in June, 14 days in Sept, 7 days at Christmas.
Admission: Members of the University only.
Enquiries: By post and telephone.
Copying: Xerox.
Lending: None.
Union Record: COLAESS, Cambridge University *Current serials.*

18 *Faculty of Modern and Medieval Languages, University of Cambridge*

Modern and Medieval Languages Libraries
Sidgwick Avenue, Cambridge CB3 9DA
Tel: Cambridge 56411 (STD code 0223)
Librarian: Miss E. L. Falconer MA

Although the libraries as a whole are concerned primarily with literature and secondly with language, there are 600 volumes of historical material among the 1,600 books in the Latin American section. Three periodicals are currently taken and about 100 books are added annually. The Latin American section was created in 1970 from books already in the Spanish section (which dates from 1918) and from new accessions.

Author catalogue and classified shelf list. Own classification. Open access.

Hrs: Mon–Fri (Full term only) 0900–2200 (–1700 during

vacations and last weeks of Summer term). Sat 0900–1300 (also 1400–1700 during first 5 weeks of Summer term). Closed during vacations, except residential period of Summer vacation.

Admission: At librarian's discretion (written application).
Enquiries: By post and telephone.
Microreading: Microfilm.
Copying: Xerox.
Lending: To members of the university and, exceptionally, through inter-library loan.
Union Record: BUCLA, Cambridge University *Current serials.*
PUBLICATIONS:
Readers' guide.

19 *Institute of Criminology, University of Cambridge*

Radzinowicz Library of Criminology
7 West Road, Cambridge CB3 9DT
Tel: Cambridge 64323 (STD code 0223)
Librarian: Miss R. Perry BA, ALA

The library is the principal criminological collection in the country, and it aims at an up-to-date and reasonably complete international coverage. It has been acquiring a limited amount of Latin American material since 1962 within its main fields of interest (penology, treatment of juveniles, criminal law). Most of this material originates from outside Latin America and relates to penal codes and systems.

Author, alphabetical subject and classified subject catalogues. Bliss classification. Open access.

Hrs: Term: Mon–Thurs 0900–1300, 1345–2200; Fri 0900–1300, 1345–1745; Sat 1000–1245. Vacations: Mon–Fri 0900–1300, 1400–1800. Closed one week at Easter and one week at Christmas.
Admission: At librarian's discretion (written application).
Enquiries: By post and telephone.
Lending: To members of the university and through inter-library loan.
Union Record: Cambridge University *Current serials.*

PUBLICATIONS:
Quarterly accessions list.
Guide and regulations.

20 Scientific Periodicals Library, University of Cambridge

Bene't Street, Cambridge CB2 3PY
Tel: Cambridge 54724 (STD code 0223)
Telex: 81240 PHILOS CAMBGE
Librarian: Miss J. E. I. Larter MA, FLA

The library, formerly the Cambridge Philosophical Library, has been collecting in the field since about 1880 and now holds 103 Latin American periodicals, almost all of which are acquired by exchange agreements. 55 of these are current. The collection includes some geography and geology relating to the region, and a small amount of archaeology, which is arranged by subject field, subdivided by country of origin.

Title and classified subject catalogues. Own classification. Closed access.

Hrs: Mon–Fri 0930–1800 (part of vacations –1700). Sat 0930–1300 (term only). Closed Late Summer bank holiday and 25–6 Dec.
Admission: At librarian's discretion (written application).
Enquiries: By post and telephone.
Microreading: Microfiche and microfilm.
Copying: Xerox.
Lending: To certain categories of members of the University, and through inter-library loan.
Union Record: BUCOP, WLSP, Cambridge University *Current serials.*

21 Scott Polar Research Institute Library, University of Cambridge

Lensfield Road, Cambridge CB2 1ER
Tel: Cambridge 66499 extn 454 (STD code 0223)
Librarian: H. G. R. V. T. D. King MA

Founded in 1920, the library has the world's most comprehensive collection on the Polar regions: books, manuscripts, maps, pamphlets, periodicals, photographs, pictures, press cuttings, and recordings. Since 1945, coverage has included Patagonia and Tierra del Fuego, as well as the Chilean and Argentine claims to Antarctic territories. Total holdings of Latin American interest amount to 100 books, 20 periodicals (mostly scientific). The library also has relevant maps and charts of Southern South America.

Author, regional and classified subject catalogues. UDC classification. Open access.

Hrs: Mon–Fri 0900–1750. Sat 0900–1245. Closed Good Fri, 25 Dec.
Admission: Bona fide researchers.
Enquiries: By post and telephone.
Microreading: Microfiche and microfilm.
Copying: Microfilm and Xerox.
Lending: Through inter-library loan.
Union Record: BUCOP, COLAESS, Cambridge University *Current serials.*

CANTERBURY

22 *University of Kent at Canterbury Library*

Canterbury, Kent. CT2 7NU
Tel: Canterbury 66822 (STD code 0227)
University Librarian: G. S. Darlow MA, ALA

The university's interest is limited to the British West Indies on which it has been collecting since 1967. It has holdings of annual reports originating in these countries, and also gives particular attention to the collection of West Indian literature in English. The collection totals about 250 volumes and 4 periodicals.

Author and classified subject catalogues. LC classification. Open access.

Hrs: Mon–Fri 0900–2100. Sat 0900–2100 (vacations –1700). Sun 1400–2100 (term only). Closed bank holidays.
Admission: At librarian's discretion (written application).
Enquiries: By post and telephone.

Microreading: Microcard, microfiche and microfilm.
Copying: Microfilm and Xerox.
Lending: To members and through inter-library loan.
Union Record: BLLD, BUCOP.
PUBLICATIONS:
Handbook.

COLCHESTER

23 *University of Essex Library*

P.O. Box 24, Wivenhoe Park, Colchester, Essex. CO4 3UA
Tel: Colchester 44144 extn 2062 (STD code 0206)
Telex: 98440 UNILIB COLCHSTR
University Librarian: P. Long MA (extn 2060)
Subject enquiries to: L. Hallewell BA, FLA (Assistant Librarian with
  responsibility for Latin American studies, extn 2383)

Essex University has offered undergraduate and postgraduate
courses with a Latin American content since its foundation in
1964, in history, linguistics, literature, politics, sociology and art.
The library, besides reflecting these interests, has also a fair
amount of material on Latin American economics, bibliography and general reference. Fringe subjects which have received some attention include the cinema, the booktrade and
Brazilian chapbooks ('literatura de cordel'), and there has been
a consistent effort to acquire Russian works on the region.
Total holdings on Latin America are about 25,000 books and
pamphlets (increasing by about 2,000 a year) and 280 periodical titles (of which about 180 are current). Regionally emphasis
has been on Brazil (8,000 titles), Chile (3,000 titles), and, more
recently, Argentina (3,000 titles). Uruguayan holdings, although
smaller (about 2,500 titles) are possibly among the most extensive in the country. The library is also making extensive acquisitions of Bolivian and Central American publications, having
been a member of the Latin American Cooperative Acquisitions
Project for Guatemala, Honduras, Nicaragua and El Salvador.
Material on the English-speaking West Indies and Guyana is
mainly literature (some 100 items). Daily newspapers are
received by sea mail from Bogotá, Buenos Aires, Caracas,

Lima, Mexico City, Rio de Janeiro, Santiago and São Paulo. Author and classified subject catalogues. LC classification. Open access.

Hrs: Term, and last week of Easter vacation: Mon–Fri 0900–2200; Sat 0900–1800; Sun 1400–1900. Remainder of vacation: Mon–Fri 0900–1730. Closed bank holidays (except Spring), and two further days at Christmas, and 2 weeks in alternate years late July/early Aug.

Admission: Bona fide enquirers (written application).

Enquiries: By post and (preferably Mon–Thurs 0900–1700) telephone and Telex.

Microreading: Microcard, microfiche and microfilm.

Copying: Microfilm and Xerox.

Typewriters: Permitted (separate room).

Lending: To members and through inter-library loan.

Union Record: BLLD (foreign language material only), BUCOP, BUCLA, COLAESS.

PUBLICATIONS:

Guide to the use of the library (annual).

Periodicals (taken by the library), 1973.

Politics, a guide to reference material held, 1972.

Social and comparative studies, a bibliography of reference material, 1969. *Supplement,* 1970.

COVENTRY

24   *University of Warwick Library*

Gibbet Hill Road, Coventry CV4 7AL

Tel: Coventry 24011 extn 2026 (STD code 0203)

Telex: 31406 UNILIB COVENTRY

University Librarian: P. E. Tucker BLITT, MA, ALA

The library began collecting material on Latin America and the Caribbean in 1964 and now has 1,100 volumes and 30 periodicals. Special emphasis has been placed since 1969 on the acquisition of economic reports and statistical material now constituting one of the largest collections of this kind in Great Britain. The material consists of duplicates from the Board of Trade Library and publications received from Argentina,

Brazil, Chile, Costa Rica, Ecuador, Haiti, Jamaica, Mexico, St Lucia and St Vincent. The collection has been built up to serve the needs of the Schools of Economics, Business and Management Studies at Warwick and to provide, on a subscription basis, a service to industry. The economic reports and statistical material are not available for loan.

Author and classified subject catalogues; title indexes for periodicals, reports and statistics. LC classification; Board of Trade classification for reports and statistics. Open access.

Hrs: Mon–Fri 0900–2130 (Aug –1730, rest of vacations –1800). Sat 0900–1800 (vacations –1230). Sun 1000–2130 (term only). Closed bank holidays (except Spring bank holiday).

Admission: At librarian's discretion (written application or SCONUL vacation reading card).

Enquiries: By post and telephone.

Microreading: Microcard, microfiche and microfilm.

Copying: Microfilm and Xerox.

Typewriters: Permitted.

Lending: To members and through inter-library loan (except as indicated above).

Union Record: BLLD (British pre-1900 and American material), BUCOP, BUCLA, WMRLS, COLAESS.

PUBLICATIONS:
Readers' guide.

DUNDEE

25 *University of Dundee Library*

Dundee, Scotland. DD1 4HN
Tel: Dundee 23181 extn 201 (STD code 0382)
Telex: 76293 UNIVLIB DUNDEE
University Librarian: J. R. Barker MA, FLA

The library's holdings of material on Latin America and the Caribbean amount to about 550 books and 10 periodicals.

Author and classified subject catalogues. Dewey classification. Open access.

Hrs: Mon–Fri 0900–2200 (vacations –1700). Sat 0900–1200.

Closed 1–2 Jan, one week at the end of June/beginning of July, 25–6 Dec, 31 Dec.
Admission: Open to general public (annual fee required).
Enquiries: By post and telephone.
Microreading: Microcard, microfiche and microfilm.
Copying: Microfilm and Xerox.
Lending: To members and through inter-library loan.
Union Record: BUCOP, SCL.
PUBLICATIONS:
Readers' guide.

EDINBURGH

26 *National Library of Scotland*

George IV Bridge, Edinburgh, Scotland. EH1 1EW
Tel: 031–225 4104
Telex: 72638 NATLIBSCOT EDIN
Librarian: E. F. D. Roberts MA, PHD
Subject enquiries to: A. M. Marchbank MA (Assistant Keeper with responsibility for Latin American materials)

The library has enjoyed copyright deposit privileges since 1710 and, as a result, has a large collection of English language material on Latin America and the Caribbean. Foreign language buying on the area became considerable only after 1945, and is carried out with due regard to the purchasing policy of Edinburgh University Library. The Library now has about 50 relevant periodical titles. Special collections include the Astorga collection of pre-1800 imprints, 21 of which are from Latin America, and the Hume collection of 140 items on Latin America (especially Chile) published between 1850 and 1920.

Author and (for books published in or after 1968) title and (for foreign books) alphabetical subject catalogues. Own classification. Closed access.

Hrs: Mon–Fri 0930–2030. Sat 0930–1300. Closed 1–2 Jan, 25 Dec.
Admission: Bona fide researchers.
Enquiries: By post.
Microreading: Microcard, microfiche and microfilm.

Copying: Microfilm and Xerox.
Typewriters: Permitted.
Lending: Through inter-library loan.
Union Record: BUCOP, BUCLA, SCL.
PUBLICATIONS:
A short-title catalogue of foreign books published up to 1600.
Weekly list of foreign accessions (available to libraries and university departments).

27 *Royal Scottish Geographical Society Library*

10 Randolph Crescent, Edinburgh, Scotland. EH3 7TU
Tel: 031–225 3330
Secretary: Donald G. Moir FRSGS
The library's collection, which relates to geography and travel, totals some 25,000 books, but it is not known what proportion of them relates to Latin America. Some of the periodicals in the collection are acquired by exchange.
  Author and classified subject catalogues. Own classification. Open access.
Hrs: Mon–Fri 1000–1700. Sat 1000–1230. Closed Scottish bank holidays and throughout August.
Admission: Open to general public.
Enquiries: By post and telephone.
Lending: To members and through inter-library loan.

28 *Royal Society of Edinburgh Library*

22 George Street, Edinburgh, Scotland. EH2 2PQ
Tel: 031–225 6057
Librarian: W. H. Rutherford FCIS, FRSE
The library consists mainly of periodical literature, particularly material emanating from scientific societies, and has relatively few books. Besides science, it has some coverage of social science, medicine, veterinary medicine and geography. It began collecting material on Latin America and the West Indies in the middle of the nineteenth century, and has some 150 periodical titles from the region. All current acquisition is through its exchange programme.

Author and title catalogues. Unclassified. Open access.

Hrs: Mon–Fri 0930–1700. Closed Scottish bank holidays.

Admission: On the recommendation of a Fellow of the Society or responsible employing authority.

Enquiries: By post and telephone.

Copying: Microfilm and Xerox.

Lending: To users and through inter-library loan.

Union Record: BUCOP.

29   University of Edinburgh Library

George Square, Edinburgh, Scotland. EH8 9LJ

Tel: 031–667 1011

University Librarian: E. R. S. Fifoot MC, MA, ALA

The university's main teaching interest arises from the needs of the course for the MA in Hispanic Studies, which includes papers on the literature and the history of Latin America. The collection contains more than 3,000 items, with more emphasis towards literature than history.

Author and classified subject catalogues. Dewey classification (modified). Open access.

Hrs: Mon–Fri 0900–2200 (vacations –1700). Sat 0900–1230 (term only). Closed 1–2 Jan, Good Fri, Edinburgh autumn holiday and 25 Dec.

Admission: At librarian's discretion (written application).

Enquiries: By post and telephone to members only.

Microreading: Microcard, microfiche and microfilm.

Copying: Microfilm and Xerox.

Lending: To members and through inter-library loan.

Union Record: BLLD, BUCOP, BUCLA, SCL.

PUBLICATIONS:

Readers' guide.

EGHAM

30   Royal Holloway College Library, University of London

Egham Hill, Egham, Surrey. TW20 0EX

Tel: Egham 4455 (STD code 07843; London area local code 389)

Librarian: R. J. E. Horrill BA

The library has been collecting material on Latin America since 1964. The collection now consists of about 500 volumes mainly on the history of Latin America and the West Indies.
Author catalogue and classified subject list. Bliss classification. Open access.

Hrs: Mon–Fri 0900–2100 (vacations –1700). Sat 0900–1300 (except Christmas and Summer vacations). Sun 1400–1800 (term only). Closed Easter, Late Summer and Christmas bank holidays and certain days adjoining.

Admission: At librarian's discretion.

Enquiries: By post (to members only) and telephone.

Microreading: Microcard, microfiche, and microfilm.

Copying: Microfilm (through University of London Library) and Xerox.

Lending: To members, and (very exceptionally) non-members, and through inter-library loan.

Union Record: BUCOP, BUCLA.

PUBLICATIONS:
Guide to the library.
Hand-list of periodicals.

EXETER

31   *Devon County Library*

Barley House, Isleworth Road, Redhills, Exeter EX4 1RQ
Tel: Exeter 74142/3 (STD code 0392)
Telex: 42933 DEVONLIB EXETER
County Librarian: R. G. Charlesworth ALA

Since 1960, the library has been responsible, under the South-West Regional Subject Specialisation Scheme, for collecting material on the topography and history of Mexico, Central America and the West Indies, as classified in the *British National Bibliography.* It has a blanket order scheme to cover such material and the collection now totals some 600 titles.

Author and classified subject catalogues. Dewey classification. Open access.

Hrs: Mon–Fri 0900–1730. Sat 0900–1200. Closed bank holidays.
Admission: Open to general public.
Enquiries: By post and telephone.
Microreading: Microcard, microfiche and microfilm.
Lending: To users (readers' tickets from other U.K. public libraries accepted), and through inter-library loan.
Union Record: BLLD, SWRLS.

32 *University of Exeter Library*

Prince of Wales Road, Exeter, Devon. EX4 4PT
Tel: Exeter 77911 (STD code 0392)
Telex: 42894 UNIVERSITY EXTR
University Librarian: J. F. Stirling MA

The library has a small collection on Latin America and the Caribbean totalling 400 books and ten periodicals, intended to support the course work of the departments.

Author and alphabetical subject catalogues. Dewey classification. Open access.

Hrs: Term: Mon–Fri 0900–2200. Sat 0900–1730. Sun 1400–1730 (small reading room only). Vacations: Mon–Fri 0900–1800 (Christmas, Easter and first and last two weeks of Summer vacation, otherwise 0900–1730). Sat 0900–1200. Closed bank holidays.
Admission: At librarian's discretion (written application).
Enquiries: By post and telephone.
Microreading: Microcard, microfiche and microfilm.
Copying: Xerox.
Lending: To members and through inter-library loan.
Union Record: BLLD, BUCOP, BUCLA, SWRLS, COLAESS.
PUBLICATIONS:
Library guide.

GLASGOW

33 *Glasgow Corporation Public Libraries*

Mitchell Library
North Street, Glasgow, Scotland. G3 7DN

Tel: 041–248 7121
Telex: 778732 LIBRARIO GLW
Librarian: C. W. Black MA, FLA

The reference library has been collecting Latin American and Caribbean material since 1877, and is strongest in English language, and more particularly British imprints. There is also a municipal lending library.

Author, alphabetical subject and classified subject catalogues. Dewey classification. Closed access.

Hrs: Mon–Sat 0930–2100. Sun (Oct–March) 1400–2000. Closed Scottish bank holidays.
Admission: Open to general public.
Enquiries: By post and telephone.
Microreading: Microcard and microfilm.
Copying: Microfilm and Xerox.
Lending: None.
Union Record: BUCOP.

PUBLICATIONS:
Catalogue of additions 1915–1949, 1952, 2 vols.

34   *Institute of Latin American Studies Library, University of Glasgow*

5 University Gardens, Glasgow, Scotland. G12 8QT
Tel: 041–339 8855 extn 545
Librarian; Miss K. M. Field BA

The Institute and its library were founded in 1966, following the university's decision to accept the invitation of the University Grants Committee to found a Parry Centre. It now consists of 5,000 volumes and 40 periodical titles. Special features of the collection are economic statistics, bank reports and literature, and the library is also comparatively strong on Brazilian material. Current acquisitions policy emphasises Brazil, Chile, Cuba and Mexico, and, with the exception of essential teaching material, consists almost entirely of recent publications. A start has been made on the collection of films, tapes and microfilms.

Author, title, alphabetical subject and regional catalogues. Own classification. Open access.

Hrs: Mon–Fri 0900–1700. Closed bank holidays (except Spring), and staff holidays.
Admission: Bona fide researchers (admissions book).
Enquiries: By post and telephone.
Copying: Xerox (through university library).
Lending: To users, and through inter-library loan.
Union Record: BUCLA.
INSTITUTE PUBLICATIONS:
Latin American Institute Occasional Papers.

35   *University of Glasgow Library*

Hillhead Street, Glasgow, Scotland. G12 8QE
Tel: 041–334 2122
Telex: 778421 GUL GLASGOW
University Librarian and Keeper of the Hunterian Books and MSS:
    R. O. MacKenna MA, ALA
Subject enquiries to: Miss E. M. Sillitto MA, ALA (Assistant
    Librarian in charge of Latin American materials)

The systematic acquisition of Latin American and Caribbean materials by the library began in 1957. Following the decision to found a Parry Centre at the university in 1965, the collection received a further impetus, and must now constitute one of the more extensive university collections in the United Kingdom, as well as being emphatically the largest in Scotland. It consists of a minimum of 10,000 works and 100 periodical titles. The library is especially strong in literature, particularly Brazilian literature, and economics.

Author and classified subject catalogues. LC classification. Open access.

Hrs: Mon–Fri 0900–2130 (vacations –1700). Sat 0900–1230.
    Closed 1–2 Jan, first two weeks of summer vacation, 25
    Dec and all Saturdays of Christmas vacation.
Admission: Bona fide researchers at the library committee's
    discretion (fee required).
Enquiries: By post and telephone.
Microreading: Microcard, microfiche and microfilm.
Copying: Xerox.
Lending: To members and (at library committee's discretion,

and on payment of a fee) non-members, and through inter-library loan.

Union Record: BLLD, BUCOP, BUCLA, SCL, COLAESS.

PUBLICATION:

Readers' guide.

36   University of Strathclyde

Andersonian Library
Richmond Street, Glasgow, Scotland. GI IXQ
Tel: 041–552 4400 extn 2249/2250
Telex: 77472 STRATHLIB GLW
University Librarian: C. G. Wood MA, FLA

The library, which began collecting on Latin America and the Caribbean in 1965, has 1,000 volumes and 12 periodical titles, with emphasis on Spanish American literature.

Author, alphabetical subject and classified subject catalogues. UDC classification. Open access.

Hrs: Mon–Fri 0900–2200 (vacations 0930–1700). Sat 0900–1730 (vacations 0930–1200). First 7 Sundays in summer term: 1400–1900. Closed Scottish bank holidays, and one week in June or July.

Admission: At librarian's discretion (fee may be required).

Enquiries: By telephone (to members only).

Microreading: Microcard, microfiche and microfilm.

Copying: Microfilm and Xerox.

Lending: To members and (at librarian's discretion) non-members, and through inter-library loan.

Union Record: BLLD, BUCLA, SCL.

GUILDFORD

37   University of Surrey Library

Stag Hill, Guildford, Surrey. GU2 5XH
Tel: Guildford 71281 (STD code 0483)
Telex: 85331 UNIV SURREY GFD
University Librarian: R. F. Eatwell FLA

The main interests of the university (formerly the Battersea

College of Advanced Technology) are natural science, technology and the social sciences. The library began collecting material on Latin America and the Caribbean in 1970 and has 300 books and 5 periodicals.
Author and classified subject catalogues. UDC classification. Open access.

Hrs: Mon–Fri 0900–2200 (vacations –1700). Sat 0900–1800. Sun 1400–1800. Closed Sat and Sun in vacations, and bank holidays (except Spring).
Admission: At librarian's discretion (visitor's book).
Enquiries: By post and telephone to members only.
Microreading: Microcard, microfiche and microfilm.
Copying: Xerox.
Lending: To members and through inter-library loan.
PUBLICATIONS:
Readers' guide.

HARPENDEN

38   *Rothamsted Experimental Station Library*

Harpenden, Herts. AL5 2JQ
Tel: Harpenden 63133 extn 71/2 (STD code 05827)
Director of the Commonwealth Bureau of Soils: W. D. Brind BSC
Librarian of the Rothamsted Experimental Station Library: T. Cawley BA, ALA

The library of the Rothamsted Experimental Station is devoted to agricultural research, especially in the fields of soil science, fertilisers, crop protection, and soil surveying. It contains 5,000 books, 8,000 pamphlets and 2,200 current periodicals, some relating to Latin America. The Commonwealth Bureau of Soils uses the collection to compile a card index relating to soils, the use of fertilisers and agricultural systems throughout the world. The card index contains about 3,000 cards referring to about 1,500 research papers on Latin America and the Caribbean, and was started in 1932. In addition to the regular preparation of the abstracting journal, *Soils and Fertilizers,* the Bureau is prepared to answer postal enquiries about topics within its field of interest.

Hrs: Mon–Fri 0900–1730. Closed bank holidays.
Admission: At librarian's discretion.
Enquiries: By post.

KINGSTON UPON HULL

39 *University of Hull*

Brynmor Jones Library
Hull, Yorks. HU6 7RX
Tel: Hull 46311 (STD code 0482)
Telex: 52530 UNILIB HULL
University Librarian: P. A. Larkin MA, HONDLITT, ALA, FRSL
Latin American holdings, built up over the last ten years,
amount to some 1,300 books and 15 periodical titles.
  Author and classified subject catalogues. LC classification.
Open access.
Hrs: Mon–Fri 0900–2200 (vacations –1750). Sat 0900–1300.
  Closed bank holidays (except Spring).
Admission: At librarian's discretion.
Enquiries: By post and telephone to members only.
Microreading: Microcard, microfiche and microfilm.
Copying: Microfilm and Xerox.
Typewriters: Permitted.
Lending: To members of the University, and through inter-
  library loan.
Union Record: BLLD, BUCOP, BUCLA, COLAESS.
PUBLICATIONS:
Readers' guide (annual).
Periodicals 1971.

LEEDS

40 *University of Leeds*

Brotherton Library
Leeds, Yorks. LS2 9JT
Tel: Leeds 31751 extn 6551 (STD code 0532)
University Librarian: D. Cox BA, ALA

Subject enquiries to: C. McCarthy BA, ALA (Assistant Librarian with responsibility for Latin American materials)

The library's Latin American holdings consist of some 2,600 books and 15 periodical titles, over half of which relate to Spanish American language and literature. Other interests include West Indian literature and sociological and rural topics especially in Bolivia and Ecuador. Acquisition of Braziliana (chiefly literature) began about 1970. About a tenth of current intake is of older material.

Author and classified subject catalogues. Own classification. Open access.

Hrs: Mon–Fri 0900–2200 (Summer vacation –1700, other vacations –2100). Sat 0900–1300 (Summer vacation –1230). Sun 1400–1900 (term only). Closed Easter and Late Summer bank holidays and the day following them, and 5 days at Christmas.

Admission: At librarian's discretion.

Enquiries: By post and telephone.

Microreading: Microcard, microfiche and microfilm.

Copying: Microfilm and Xerox.

Lending: To members and through inter-library loan.

Union Record: BLLD, BUCOP, BUCLA, COLAESS.

PUBLICATIONS:

R. Offor, *A descriptive guide to the libraries of the University of Leeds,* 1947. *Supplement,* 1949.

LEICESTER

41 *Leicestershire County Library*

Clarence Street, Leicester LE1 3RN
Tel: Leicester 22012 (STD code 0533)
Telex: 34307 BOOKINFO LESTER
Librarian: G. E. Smith FLA

The library has 605 books, mostly of a general nature, relating to Latin America and the Caribbean, a few music scores, and some 40 gramophone records. There is a small collection of relevant juvenilia and the library also has a few films, wall charts and film strips for the use of schools and other educational institutions in the area.

Author, title and classified subject catalogues. Dewey classification. Open access.

Hrs: Mon–Fri 0900–1730. Sat 0900–1700. Closed bank holidays and Tuesday following Easter, Spring and Late Summer bank holidays.
Admission: Open to general public.
Enquiries: By post and telephone.
Microreading: Microfilm.
Copying: Xerox.
Lending: To users (readers' tickets from other U.K. public libraries accepted) and through inter-library loan.
Union Record: BLLD, EMRLS.

42   University of Leicester Library

University Road, Leicester LEI 7RH
Tel: Leicester 50000 (STD code 0533)
Telex: 341198 UNIVLIB LESTER
University Librarian: D. G. F. Walker MA, LLB

The library has a small collection on Latin America and the Caribbean with perhaps 500 books and 10 periodicals, and subscribes to the publications of the Organization of American States.

Author, part title and classified subject catalogues. Dewey classification. Open access.

Hrs: Mon–Fri 0900–2300 (vacations –1730). Sat 0900–1800 (vacations –1230). Sun 1500–2100 (term only). Closed bank holidays.
Admission: At librarian's discretion (written application).
Enquiries: By post and telephone.
Microreading: Microcard, microfiche and microfilm.
Copying: Xerox.
Lending: To users and through inter-library loan.
Union Record: BLLD, BUCOP, BUCLA, EMRLS, COLAESS.
PUBLICATIONS:
Guide to the library.

LIVERPOOL

43 *Liverpool City Libraries*

William Brown Street, Liverpool L3 8EW
Tel: 051–207 2147
Telex: 62500 LADSIRLAC LPOOL
Librarian:

The City's library system, in particular the International and Commonwealth Libraries, has a strong English language collection on Latin America and the Caribbean totalling 8,000 volumes and 15 periodicals, and a smaller collection of imaginative literature in Spanish and Portuguese. Other subject departments, such as the Commercial, Technical and Art departments also contain relevant material. Liverpool's extensive commercial and cultural relations with Latin America are given special emphasis.

Author, title, alphabetical subject and classified subject catalogues. Dewey classification. Open access.

Hrs: Mon–Fri 0900–2100. Sat 0900–1700. Closed bank holidays.
Admission: Open to general public.
Enquiries: By post and telephone.
Microreading: Microcard and microfilm. (Microfiche reader restricted to staff use.)
Copying: Microfilm and Xerox.
Lending: To users and through inter-library loan.
Union Record: BUCOP, COLAESS, North West union list of periodicals.

PUBLICATIONS:
Guide to the Central libraries.
Liverpool City Libraries catalogues (published periodically).

44 *University of Liverpool Library*

P.O. Box 123, Liverpool L69 3DA
Tel: 051–709 6022
Telex: 627095 UNIVERSITY LPL
University Librarian: D. H. Varley, MA, DIPLIB, FLA

The library began collecting material on Latin America and

the Caribbean in the early twentieth century but significant acquisitions were made only after the establishment of a Parry Centre at the University in 1965. The library now has 14,150 books and 300 periodical titles, of which 70 are currently received. In and after 1975 the bulk of the collection in the humanities and social sciences, at present in the Harold Cohen Library and Arts Reading Room respectively, will be housed in the new Sydney Jones Library building; scientific holdings will be concentrated mainly in the Harold Cohen and associated libraries, as at present. Special emphasis is given in the collection to Peru (all aspects), Brazil (literature, politics, sociology, economics and geography), and to the following topics in general: agrarian reform, literature and history. There is also a current emphasis on census data, and Chilean politics and sociology.

Author and (partially completed) classified subject catalogues. LC classification. Open access.

Hrs: Mon–Fri 0900–2130 (Easter vacation –1800 or (certain sections) -2130. Summer vacation –1700. Christmas vacation –1800). Sat 0900–1300. Closed bank holidays

Admission: At librarian's discretion (letter of recommendation or SCONUL vacation reading card).

Enquiries: By post and telephone.

Microreading: Microcard, microfiche and microfilm.

Copying: Microfilm and Xerox.

Typewriters: By arrangement.

Lending: To members and through inter-library loan.

Union Record: BLLD, BUCLA, COLAESS, North West union list of periodicals.

PUBLICATIONS:
Notes for readers.

LONDON

45 *Anglo-Chilean Society Library*

12 Devonshire Street, London WIN 2DS
Tel: 01–580 1271
Secretary: W. R. Smithson
The Society has been collecting material since 1944 and now

has 400 volumes. Books by Chilean authors constitute the major feature of the collection. Material is added only intermittently, and is predominantly non-current.

No catalogue. Unclassified. Open access.

Hrs: At Secretary's discretion (prior application).
Admission: Open to general public.
Enquiries: By post and telephone.
Lending: To members and to recommended non-members.

46 Bank of England

Reference Library
Threadneedle Street, London EC2R 8AH
Tel: 01–601 4846 and 01–601 4715
Librarian: G. O. Randle BCOM

The library's coverage is principally in banking, especially central banking, but there is some general statistical, trade and other economic material. Some periodical holdings are complete from the late 1920s but most date from 1945. Currently 91 periodicals relating to Latin America are regularly received, but many are not retained permanently.

Author, alphabetical subject, and classified subject catalogues. Dewey classification (extended and modified). Open access.

Hrs: Mon–Fri 0930–1730. Closed bank holidays.
Admission: Bona fide researchers (prior written application).
Enquiries: By post.
Microreading: Microfilm.
Copying: Xerox (by arrangement).
Lending: At librarian's discretion.
PUBLICATIONS: (circulated within the bank and to other central banks):
List of additions (monthly).

47 Bedford College Library, University of London

Regent's Park, London NW1 4NS
Tel: 01–486 4400 extn 333
Librarian: G. M. Paterson BA, ALA

The library has been collecting on Latin America since 1965, and now has 750 items. The collection is devoted entirely to geography, and there is a special interest in the physical and ecological geography of tropical Latin America.

Author and classified subject catalogues. Dewey classification. Open access.

Hrs: Mon–Fri 0900–2100 (vacations –1700). Sat 0900–1300. Closed bank holidays.
Admission: At librarian's discretion (prior written application).
Enquiries: By post and telephone.
Microreading: Microfilm.
Copying: Xerox.
Lending: To members and through inter-library loan.
Union Record: BLLD, BUCOP, BUCLA, COLAESS.
PUBLICATIONS:
Guide to the library.

48   *Board of Inland Revenue Library*

New Wing, Somerset House, London WC2R 1LB
Tel: 01–836 2407 extn 325
Librarian: R. F. Knight
Subject enquiries to: J. Rodway (Foreign Intelligence, Room 11, extn 455)

The library, which has been collecting on Latin America since 1940, now has 1,000 items relating to the area, mainly in the field of direct taxation legislation. In addition to purchasing any relevant material which comes to light, the library benefits from exchange agreements with some governments, and maintains some loose leaf publications in current condition.

Author, title, alphabetical subject and classified subject catalogues. UDC classification. Open access.

Hrs: Mon–Fri 0900–1700. Closed bank holidays.
Admission: At librarian's discretion (prior application).
Enquiries: By post and telephone.
Copying: Xerox.
Lending: None.

49 *Brazilian Embassy Library/Biblioteca da Embaixada do Brasil*

32 Green Street, London WIY 4AT
Tel: 01–629 0155
Librarian: Miss O. V. Vesentini (extn 68)
The Embassy library was begun in 1963 mainly to provide commercial information, economic reports, statistics and similar material. Recently it has become the Cultural Attaché's responsibility, and its emphasis has moved towards Brazilian culture, literature, including children's literature, art, and history. Attention is also paid to the legal and diplomatic needs of embassy staff, for example, a complete set of Brazilian national laws and statutes (from 1808), and Brazilian Foreign Office annual reports (from 1857) are held. Holdings are mainly, though not exclusively, Brazilian publications and amount to 6,500 books and pamphlets, and 50 periodical titles (including some daily newspapers), 20 films (16 mm, up to 60 minutes long), together with slides, photographs and maps.

Author and alphabetical subject catalogues. UDC classification. Open access.

Hrs: Mon–Fri 1000–1300, 1500–1800. Closed English bank holidays and Brazilian national holidays (1 Jan, Mon and Tues before Ash Wed, 21 Apr, 1 May, 7 Sep, 15 Nov).
Admission: Open to general public.
Enquiries: Preferably by post.
Lending: To general public (on written application and at Cultural Attaché's discretion) and through inter-library loan.
Union Record: BLLD (very partial), BUCLA. Holdings also notified to Hispanic and Luso-Brazilian Council (Canning House) Library (no. 72).

50 *British Broadcasting Corporation*

BBC Music Library
Yalding House, 156 Great Portland Street, London WIN 6AJ
Tel: 01–580 4468
Telex: 22182 BBC LONDON
Librarian: Miss M. Miller

The library has a few items (for example a dozen books, and the scores of some songs) of Latin American interest, and receives the Organization of American States' *Composers of the Americas* as a source of biographical detail for obtaining works as and when required.

Author and title catalogues. Closed access.

Hrs: Mon–Fri 0930–1730. Closed bank holidays.
Admission: BBC staff and broadcasters only.
Enquiries: By post and telephone.
Microreading: Microfilm.
Copying: Xerox.
Lending: To broadcasters, and (very exceptionally) through inter-library loan.

PUBLICATIONS:
BBC catalogues of chamber music, choral music, organ music, piano music and songs.

51 *British Council English-Teaching Information Centre (ETIC) and Centre for Information on Language Teaching and Research (CILT)*

Language-Teaching Library
State House, 63 High Holborn, London WC1R 4SZ
Tel: 01–242 9020 extn 782
Librarian: Mrs J. O. Howard BA, FLA

The ETIC library, created by the British Council in 1961, and primarily concerned with the teaching of English as a foreign language, became in 1966 the joint library of the ETIC and the newly formed CILT, which is concerned with modern language teaching in the United Kingdom. The English section includes studies of overseas varieties of English, and a very large collection of textbooks (many published abroad) for teaching English as a second language. In the Spanish section, there are 360 books and 6 periodical titles which refer to American Spanish. There is, in addition, a very small Portuguese section. A separate audio-visual section has a wide selection of sets of teaching materials in various languages.

Author, title and classified subject catalogues. Own classification. Open access.

Hrs: Mon, Tues, Thur 0930–1730. Wed 0930–2000. Fri 0930–
1700. Closed bank holidays.
Admission: Open to general public.
Enquiries: By post and telephone.
Microreading: Microfiche and microfilm.
Copying: Xerox.
Lending: None except general education books and some
duplicate language, language-teaching and textbook materi-
als to users and through inter-library loan.

PUBLICATIONS:

A language teaching bibliography, 2nd edn, Cambridge, Cambridge
University Press, 1972.
Language teaching abstracts, Cambridge, Cambridge University
Press, 1967– (quarterly).

52   *British Film Institute*

National Film Archive
81 Dean Street, London WIV 6AA
Tel: 01–437 4355
Telex: 27624 BRIFILINST LDN
Head of Information Department: Miss B. Davies
Librarian: Miss G. Hartnoll FLA

The Institute has been interested in the Latin American cinema
since the 1940s. The National Film Archive has 10 feature
films and 9 documentaries. Its Book Library and Information
Department has about 30 books, 6 current periodicals, and
some newspaper cuttings and publicity material.

Author, title and classified subject catalogues. UDC classification (modified). Closed access.

Hrs: Mon 1400–1800. Tues, Fri 1000–1800. Wed–Thur 1000–
2100. Closed bank holidays.
Admission: Members only (one month visitor membership
£0.82).
Enquiries: By post and telephone.
Microreading: Microfiche and microfilm.
Copying: Xerox.
Lending: To members and through inter-library loan.

53   *British Institute of Recorded Sound Library*

29 Exhibition Road, London sw7 2AS
Tel: 01–589 6603
Director: P. Saul

Since 1948, the Institute has been collecting records, tape recordings, and record catalogues, together with books and periodicals in any language on non-technical aspects of recorded sound. Its Latin American holdings include 70 discs of literature, about 40 hours of tape recordings of folk music, and numerous discs of folk and composed music.

No catalogue (but computerised catalogue currently being considered). Closed access.

Hrs: Mon–Fri 1000–1330, 1430–1800. Closed bank holidays.
Admission: Bona fide researchers.
Enquiries: By post and telephone.
Microreading: Microfilm.
Copying: Xerox.
Lending: None.
PUBLICATIONS:
B. Moser and D. Tayler, *The music of some Indian tribes of Colombia* (3 LP discs with text and photographs), 1973.
Recorded sound (quarterly journal), 1961–.

54   *British Library: Newspaper Library*

Colindale Avenue, Colindale, London NW9 5HE
Tel: 01–205 6039; 01–205 4788
Superintendent: P. E. Allen BA

Formerly the newspaper library of the British Museum, the British Library Newspaper Library at Colindale holds the national reference collection of newspapers, except for those published in London before 1800 which are held at the British Library Reference Division in Great Russell Street, London (no. 55). In addition to the newspapers of former British possessions, some 18 titles are received currently from the rest of Latin America. But older materials form a predominant part of current purchases, so that the total number of Latin American titles held is in the region of a thousand, and the oldest of these date from the early nineteenth century. Some are microfilm copies.

Alphabetical and geographical title catalogues. Closed access.

Hrs: Mon–Sat 1000–1700 (no admission after 1615). Closed Good Fri, one week starting the first Mon in May and 24–6 Dec.

Admission: Bona fide researchers of 21 or over (written application and recommendation). British Library Reference Division (Bloomsbury) Reading Room tickets admit to the library. Only short period tickets (for up to 6 days) are issued at Colindale.

Enquiries: By post and telephone.

Microreading: Microfilm.

Copying: Microfilm, photocopy and Xerox.

Typewriters (and tape-recorders): Permitted (separate room).

Lending: None.

55 *British Library, Reference Division (British Museum Library)*

Great Russell Street, London WC1B 3DG

Tel: 01–636 1555

Telex: 21462 BRITMUSLIB LDN

Director-General of the British Library Reference Division: D. T. Richnell CBE, BA, FLA

Subject enquiries to: H. G. Whitehead (Assistant Keeper with part time responsibility for materials in the Spanish and Portuguese languages, extn 421); D. Mackenzic (Assistant Keeper in the Italian and Hispanic Language Group, extn 355)

Although it has no collection specifically devoted to Latin America, the British Museum Library, which now constitutes the Reference Division of the British Library has undoubtedly the largest and most significant holdings on the area in the British Isles, and has been collecting material since its foundation in 1753. The library has material on most topics and periods, and seeks to develop an all round collection. In addition to its holdings of British imprints, received by copyright deposit, it has a particularly good collection of early Mexican and Peruvian books, and strong holdings on the independence movements of the early nineteenth century. Its collections on Mexico and Brazil are particularly noteworthy, with official documents of the period 1820–50 being especially well represented. The library takes well over 600 serials from Latin America, and subscribes to 18 newspapers which are kept in the Newspaper Library at Colindale (no. 54). Government publications are well represented in the State Papers Room, and include when possible the publications of member states of federal systems. Many older government and other official publications originally received in British government departmental libraries have been transferred to the Museum. As the national collection, the library is also outstandingly strong in materials on the former British colonies in the Caribbean and on the mainland of Latin America. In the current acquisitions programme, most emphasis is given to the River Plate countries, Mexico, Chile, Venezuela and Brazil, and then to Peru, Colombia and Bolivia. With the possible exception of Costa Rica, Central America is less well covered. About half the material at present being acquired is non-current. There is some use of exchange agreements though these have proved very difficult to negotiate. The library also has a very extensive collection of postage stamps. The holdings of the National Reference Library of Science and Invention, which is part of the British Library Reference Division, are described in entry number 56. The library of the British Museum (Natural History), which has not been incorporated into the British Library, but remains part of the British Museum, is described in entry number 57.

Author and alphabetical subject catalogues. Own classification. Closed access.

Hrs: Mon, Fri–Sat 0900–1700. Tues–Thur 0900–2100. Closed Good Fri, 24–6 Dec, and one week starting first Mon in May.

Admission: Bona fide researchers over 21 (recommendation required). Annually renewable or short-term study tickets issued according to need.

Enquiries: By post and telephone.

Microreading: Microcard, microfiche and microfilm.
Copying: Microfilm and Xerox.
Typewriters: Permitted.
Lending: None.
Union Record: BUCOP, BUCLA, COLAESS.

PUBLICATIONS:

General catalogue of printed books. Complete to the end of 1955, London, Mansell, 1960–6, 263 vols. *Ten year supplement. 1956–65,* London, Mansell, 1966, 50 vols. *Five year supplement. 1966–70,* London, Mansell, 1971, 26 vols.

Subject Index (separate sequences for 1881–1900, 1901–5, 1906–10, 1911–15, Books relating to the First World War 1914–18, 1916–20, 1921–5, 1926–30, 1931–5, 1936–40 are now all out of print). *1941–1945,* 1953. *1946–1950,* 1961 (repr. 1968), 4 vols. *1956–60,* 1966, 6 vols. (1951–5 and 1961–70 in preparation.)

Short-title catalogue of Spanish, Spanish-American and Portuguese books printed before 1601, 1921 (repr. 1966).

(These are the titles most immediately relevant to the student of Latin America.)

56 *British Library, Reference Division: Science Reference Library (SRL) (formerly National Reference Library of Science and Invention (NRLSI))*

Bayswater Branch
10 Porchester Gardens, Queensway, London W2 4DE
Tel: 01–727 3022
Telex: 22717 SCI REF B
Holborn Branch
25 Southampton Buildings, Chancery Lane, London WC2A 1AW
Tel: 01–405 8721
Telex: 266959 SCI REF H
Director: M. W. Hill MA, BSC, ARIC
Subject enquiries to: Mrs M. J. Landau (assistant in charge of Latin American acquisitions. Bayswater branch, extn 34)

The SRL is based on the former Patent Office Library which was founded in 1855 to stimulate developments in the field of invention. The scope has been widened to include developments and discoveries in any branch of the natural sciences and technology. It now forms a part of the Reference Division of the British Library. The Latin American collection is not kept separate and constitutes only a minor part of the overall collection. It consists of about 250 books in the Holborn and Bayswater branches combined and about 450 periodicals. About 25 atlases are held at Bayswater. Extensive collections of Latin American patents and trade mark journals are held at Holborn; Bayswater and Holborn together cover the other types of literature. All holdings are at research level. In respect of books published in Latin America, the SRL acquires only those on which the country is recognised as having specialised knowledge, in addition to books on the zoology, botany, agriculture and geology of each country. Latin American periodicals are acquired in so far as they fall within the library's general field of interest and are of high enough quality.

Alphabetical name and classified subject catalogues. Own classification. Mainly open access at Holborn; closed access at Bayswater.

Hrs: Mon–Fri 0930–2100 (Bayswater –1730). Sat 1000–1300 (Holborn only). Closed bank holidays.
Admission: Open to general public.
Enquiries: By post, telephone and Telex.
Microreading: Microcard, microfiche and microfilm.
Copying: Xerox. Copies from microforms can be made.
Typewriters: Permitted.
Lending: None.
Union Record: BUCOP, BUCLA, COLAESS (Holborn only), Chemical Abstracts.
PUBLICATIONS:
Guide to the NRLSI.
Aids to readers.
Periodical news (every 4 weeks).
Notes to readers.
NRLSI news.
Periodical publications in the NRLSI (set of handlists).
Occasional publications.

57 British Museum (Natural History) Library

Cromwell Road, London SW7 5BD
Tel: 01–589 6323
Librarian: M. J. Rowlands FLA

The library has been collecting in the Latin American field since its foundation in 1880, and though the material is not kept separate, and constitutes only a minor part of the library's collection, there are now between 2,000 and 3,000 volumes and between 300 and 500 periodical titles. The holdings are restricted to items containing natural history subjects, including anthropology. The library is strong in scientific reports of voyages and expeditions which concern flora and fauna. The collection is being actively developed, and particular emphasis is given to the acquisition of periodicals which contain natural history subject matter of a reasonably high standard. Most of the material acquired is current. Use is made of exchange agreements with Latin American institutions, and much material is donated to the library as a result of co-operation between the scientific staff of the Museum and kindred organisations in Latin America.

Author and classified subject catalogues. UDC classification for subject catalogue and shelf arrangement in Botany and Mineralogy. Own classification for the rest. Closed access.

Hrs: Mon–Sat 1000–1700. Closed bank holidays.
Admission: At librarian's and keepers' discretion (written application). Reader's ticket required for regular use.
Enquiries: By post and telephone.
Microreading: Microfiche and microfilm.
Copying: Xerox.
Typewriters: Permitted.
Lending: None.
Union Record: BUCOP, WLSP, COLAESS.
PUBLICATIONS:
Catalogue of the library of the British Museum (Natural History), 1903–40, 8 vols.
List of accessions to the library of the British Museum (Natural History), 6 issues a year.

58 *British Numismatic Society Library*

Warburg Institute, Woburn Square, London WC1H OAB
Tel: (Warburg Institute): 01–580 9663
Honorary Librarian: R. H. Thompson ALA

The library of the British Numismatic Society (founded 1904, and combined with that of the Royal Numismatic Society, founded 1837) is not concerned with Spanish America or Brazil, but holds a small amount of material relevant to the former British West Indies. The Royal Numismatic Society collection covers all countries and periods though little material is in fact held on the areas covered by the directory.

Author catalogue. Own classification. Open access.

Hrs: Mon–Fri 1000–1800. Sat (except Aug and Sept) 1000–1300. Closed bank holidays, one week at Easter and one week at Christmas.

Admission: At the discretion of the librarian of the Warburg Institute.

Enquiries: By post.

Copying: Xerox.

Lending: To members.

Union Record: Copy of catalogue at British Museum Department of Coins and Medals.

PUBLICATIONS:
Library accessions listed in *British Numismatic Journal.*

59 *Catholic Central Library (Franciscan Friars of the Atonement)*

47 Francis Street, London SW1P 1QR
Tel: 01–834 6128
Librarian: Mrs M. Buck

The library was founded in 1959. Its general collection includes a small number of books in English concerning the Church and Christian sociology in Latin America.

Author, title, alphabetical subject and classified subject catalogues. Dewey classification. Predominantly open access.

Hrs: Mon–Fri 1030–1830. Sat 1030–1630. Closed bank holidays and Sat preceding Mon bank holiday.
Admission: At librarian's discretion.
Enquiries: By post and telephone.
Copying: Xerox.
Lending: To members and through inter-library loan.
Union Record: BLLD.
PUBLICATIONS:
Quarterly supplement of new additions to stock.

60 *Chartered Institute of Transport Library*

80 Portland Place, London WIN 4DP
Tel: 01–580 5216
Librarian: Mrs J. F. O. Southgate BA, ALA

Founded in 1926, and formerly the Institute of Transport, the Chartered Institute has in its library a total stock of some 15,000 books and pamphlets and 300 periodicals, and emphasises the economic, commercial and administrative rather than the engineering aspects of transport. Latin American holdings are very small but include annual reports of transport undertakings.

Author and classified subject catalogues. Own classification. Open access.

Hrs: Mon–Fri 1000–1700. Closed bank holidays.
Admission: Bona fide researchers.
Enquiries: By post and telephone.
Copying: Xerox.
Lending: To members.
PUBLICATIONS:
Handbook.
Bibliographies.

61 *Chartered Insurance Institute Library*

20 Aldermanbury, London EC2V 7HY
Tel: 01–606 3835 extn 21/2
Librarian: A. J. Lee BA, ALA

Since about 1947 the library has been collecting material on insurance in Latin America, published in the United Kingdom and in the countries of origin. Acquisition is by standing orders, supplemented by exchange arrangements. The holdings amount to about 100 books and pamphlets, 20 periodicals and directories, and a considerable collection of newspaper cuttings.

Author, classified subject and geographical catalogues and cuttings catalogue. Own classification. Closed access.

Hrs: Mon–Fri 1000–1800 (–1930 on Mon, Tues, Wed from 1 Oct to end of Spring examinations in April). Closed bank holidays.

Admission: At librarian's discretion (recommendation required).

Enquiries: By post and telephone.

Copying: Xerox.

Lending: To members and through inter-library loan.

Union Record: BUCOP, COLAESS.

62   Church Missionary Society Library

157 Waterloo Road, London SE1 8UU
Tel: 01–928 8681 extn 129
Librarian: Miss J. M. Woods ALA

The library began collecting in the Latin American field in the nineteenth century and now has about 150 volumes relating to the area in its collection of 20,000 volumes. Two missionary magazines are also taken. The collection is an almost static one, since the Society is no longer active in the area in question.

Author, title and alphabetical subject catalogues. Dewey classification. Open access.

Hrs: Mon–Fri 0930–1700. Closed bank holidays.

Admission: At librarian's discretion (written application).

Enquiries: By post and telephone.

Lending: To users, and through inter-library loan.

Union Record: BLLD.

63   Commonwealth Institute Library

Kensington High Street, London W8 6NQ
Tel: 01–602 3252 extn 127
Librarian: M. Foster FLA
Subject enquiries to: R. Hughes ALA (Assistant Librarian)

The library has been collecting material on the Commonwealth West Indies, Guyana and Belize (British Honduras) since 1962, and has between 800 and 1,000 volumes and 40 periodical titles which are shelved together. The library has a special interest in the imaginative literature of the Commonwealth countries, and material in this field, and on the arts in general, features prominently in an active acquisitions programme, which is directed entirely at current material. Contacts with the High Commissions, and with universities, are methods of supply which supplement the use of specialist book agents. Notable features of the acquisitions are the collection of juvenilia, slides, films, discs, tapes, pamphlets and charts.

Author, title and classified subject catalogues. Bliss classification. Open access.

Hrs: Mon–Sat 1000–1730. Closed bank holidays.
Admission: Open to general public.
Enquiries: By post and telephone.
Copying: Xerox.
Typewriters: Permitted.
Lending: To members and through inter-library loan.
Union Record: BLLD, BUCOP.
PUBLICATIONS:
Selected reading lists for each Commonwealth country and for certain topics.

64   *Commonwealth Secretariat Library*

10 Carlton House Terrace, London SW1Y 5HX
Tel: 01–839 3411 extns 233 and 232
Librarian: Miss M. E. Moody ALA

The Commonwealth Secretariat library dates from 1966, is particularly strong in trade and economics statistical material, and has exchange agreements with most Latin American countries.

Partial author and alphabetical subject catalogues. Unclassified. Open access.

Hrs: Mon–Fri 0915–1715. Closed bank holidays.
Admission: Members only.

Enquiries: By post and telephone.
Lending: To members, and through inter-library loan.

65 *Corporation of London, City Business Library*

Gillett House, 55 Basinghall Street, London EC2V 5BX
Tel: 01–638 8215/6
Telex: 887955 CITYLIBRARY LDN
Librarian: M. J. Campbell ALA

The library was formed in 1970 from material transferred from the Corporation's Guildhall Library. Since its aim is to provide up-to-date information to businessmen, older material is continually discarded, so that the rate of growth is moderate. Current holdings of Latin American interest are some 200 books, 300 pamphlets and 38 periodical titles. Although this includes only one newspaper (*La Prensa* of Buenos Aires), the library does take a world-wide selection of daily and Sunday papers which includes several with good Latin American coverage, such as *Le Monde* and *The New York Times*. The collection emphasises commercial directories (including telephone and Telex directories), statistics, economic background material and information on trading conditions. Much of this is received from banks, chambers of commerce and similar institutions. All publications of the Economist Intelligence Unit are obtained and the library has a block subscription to Business International Publications. Although the library's objects overlap to some extent those of the Department of Trade and Industry's Statistics and Market Intelligence library (no. 67), users may well find that in their Latin American provision they complement more than they duplicate each other.

Author and classified subject catalogues. Dewey classification, with own classification for directories and periodicals. Open access.

Hrs: Mon–Fri 0930–1730. Closed bank holidays.
Admission: Open to general public.
Enquiries: By post, telephone and Telex.
Microreading: Microfiche.
Copying: Xerox.
Lending: None.

Union Record: BLLD, BUCOP, LASER, COLAESS.
PUBLICATIONS:
Brochures on services provided.
Lists of newspapers and periodicals.

66 *Department of Trade and Industry*

Central Library
1 Victoria Street, London SWIH OET
Tel: 01–222 7877 extn 3125
Telex: 918779 DTI LIBRARY LDN
Librarian: K. A. Mallaber FLA

The library, founded in 1836 as the Board of Trade library, collects current books, periodicals and other information on the economic affairs of all Latin American countries, mostly in English. The coverage is wide rather than deep. The material is not retained permanently but is replaced as more up-to-date publications are obtained. A special feature of the library is the following sets of publications which contain some important Latin American material and which are almost certainly the only complete copies in the country available for inter-library loan:

(i) *House of Lords and House of Commons Papers* from 1801. These contain a great deal of material such as diplomatic and commercial correspondence, treaties, consular reports (1854–1920) and other documentation.

(ii) *Overseas economic surveys,* 1920–56. These superseded the pre-1920 Consular and Diplomatic Reports on commercial, economic and social conditions of foreign countries.

(iii) *Board of Trade Journal* (1886–1969) and its successor *Trade and Industry* (from 1970). This contains many reports on trading opportunities, tariff changes, changes in local legislation and regulations, etc. for all foreign countries.

(iv) *International Customs Journal* from 1891. Published by the International Customs Tariffs Bureau, Brussels, this is probably the only complete set in the U.K. It contains full texts of all customs tariffs, translated into English, for all countries. The library also holds a complete set of current legislation of Commonwealth countries. The Translators' Library has a large selection of foreign language dictionaries. Neither of these categories of material may be borrowed.

Author and alphabetical subject catalogues. LC classification. Closed access (except by special arrangement).

Hrs: Mon–Fri 0900–1730. Closed bank holidays.

Admission: At librarian's discretion (application in writing or by telephone).

Enquiries: By post and telephone.

Microreading: Microcard, microfiche and microfilm.

Copying: Microfilm and Xerox.

Lending: Through inter-library loan.

Union Record: BLLD, BUCOP, COLAESS.

67 *Department of Trade and Industry, Statistics and Market Intelligence Library*

Export House, 50 Ludgate Hill, London EC4M 7HU
Tel: 01–248 5757 extn 368
Telex: 886143 DTI EXPORT LDN
Librarian: F. Cochrane FLA, DGA

The library aims to collect all countries' statistical publications on foreign trade, industrial production, distribution, national accounts and other economic statistics, as well as general statistical abstracts and bulletins, and the reports of population censuses. Statistical publications from international organisations (including those concerned with Latin America) are also held. The official statistical sources are supplemented whenever practicable by non-official sources. The library also acquires some material of lesser interest to the Department, such as statistics of agriculture, building and finance. Publications are obtained from all Latin American countries, although the amount of detail and its currency varies from country to country. Statistical yearbooks and bulletins are received from all countries in the area. In its field, the library seeks to be the most up-to-date and comprehensive in the United Kingdom. Statistical material from abroad is retained for 15 years only, after which it is transferred to the British Museum State Paper Room, except for international publications which are filed permanently. Statistical material is on closed access, but the library has an extensive open access collection of Latin American trade and telephone directories, development plans and pamphlet material. In this respect similar and complementary provision (with the exception of development plans) also exists in the Corporation of London City Business Library (no. 65). Total Latin American holdings are about 2,000 books and 350 periodicals.

Author, title and alphabetical subject catalogues. Own classification. Access details above.

Hrs: Mon–Fri 0900–1730. Closed bank holidays.
Admission: Open to general public.
Enquiries: By post, and telephone. Requests for statistics to be extracted from overseas publications should be made to the D.T.I.'s Statistics Division (Foreign and Commonwealth Division) at the same address (tel. extn 337); this service is charged for according to the amount of staff time involved.
Copying: Xerox.
Typewriters: Available.
Other facilities: Adding machines available. Storage lockers may be rented.
Lending: None.
Union Record: BLLD.
PUBLICATIONS:
Descriptive brochure (see also the article in *Trade and industry* 20, 10, 1971, pp. 186–8).
National statistical offices of overseas countries (annual).

68   *Ealing Technical College Library*

St Mary's Road, Ealing w5 5RF
Tel: 01–579 4111 extn 246/248
Woodlands Avenue, Acton w3 9DN
Tel: 01–992 6944
Librarian: R. A. Thomas FLA, DMA

The Library began collecting in the field in 1969 to support a newly developing teaching programme, and has 260 books and 8 periodical titles on Latin America, constituting a minor part of the whole collection, and concentrated at St Mary's Road.

Author and classified subject catalogues. Dewey classification.
Open access.
Hrs: Mon–Fri 0915–2100 (vacations 0930–1630). Sat 1000–
1600 (term only). Closed bank holidays.
Admission: At librarian's discretion.
Enquiries: By post and telephone.
Microreading: Microfiche and microfilm.
Copying: Xerox.
Lending: To members, and (exceptionally) non-members, and
through inter-library loan.
Union Record: BUCOP.
PUBLICATIONS:
General library guide.
General periodical holding list.

69   *Folklore Society Library*

c/o University College, Gower Street, London WC1E 6BT
Tel: 01–387 5894
Librarian: Miss K. Hedberg BA
Subject enquiries to: Mrs D. M. C. Tanner BSC(SOC) (Assistant
Librarian)

It is not known when the Society began to collect in the
Latin American field, but its present collection amounting to
100 volumes, constitutes only a minor part of the Society's
total library. Seven periodicals are also taken. The Society's
quarterly journal *Folklore* is used to acquire some Latin American periodicals by exchange.

Author and classified subject catalogues. Own classification.
Open access.
Hrs: Mon–Fri 1000–2100 (vacations –1700). Closed bank
holidays and one week at Christmas and one week at
Easter.
Admission: Open to general public.
Enquiries: By post and telephone.
Copying: Xerox.
Lending: To members, and through inter-library loan.
Union Record: BLLD, BUCOP.

70　*Foreign and Commonwealth Office (FCO), Library and Records Department*

Sanctuary Buildings, Great Smith Street, London SW1P 3BZ
Tel: 01–839 7010 extns 263 and 268
Librarian: Miss E. C. Blayney ALA

The FCO was formed in 1968 when the Commonwealth Office (formerly the Colonial and Commonwealth Relations Offices) and the Foreign Office were amalgamated. In 1970, the Ministry of Overseas Development became a part of the FCO as the Overseas Development Administration. The Library is strong in treaties, in international law and in official publications acquired by exchange agreements with Commonwealth and some foreign governments. Other printed material for which the library is notable includes early works on travel and exploration, on modern Cuba and on the former British colonies in the West Indies. Current acquisitions policy emphasises economic development as well as foreign relations. There is also a map collection, a collection of colonial and Commonwealth postage stamps, and a small collection of photographs of the former British colonies in the West Indies.

Author, partial title, alphabetical subject and classified subject catalogues. LC and Dewey modified classification. Closed access.

Hrs: Mon–Fri 0930–1730. Closed bank holidays.
Admission: Open to general public.
Enquiries: By post and telephone.
Microreading: Microfilm.
Copying: Xerox (for staff only).
Lending: To FCO staff, and (to a limited extent) through interlibrary loan.
Union Record: BLLD (in part).

PUBLICATIONS:

New books list (monthly).
Technical cooperation (a monthly bibliography).
Catalogue of the Colonial Office Library, Boston, Mass., G. K. Hall, 1964, 15 vols.

Catalogue of the Foreign Office Library, 1926–1968, Boston, Mass., G. K. Hall, 1972, 8 vols.

71 *Heythrop College Library, University of London*

11–13 Cavendish Square, London WIM OAN
Tel: 01–580 6941
Librarian: M. J. Walsh, MA, ALA

Heythrop College was incorporated in 1971 as a non-grant receiving school of the University of London in the Faculty of Theology. Its library of 150,000 volumes is supplemented by the 50,000 volumes of the library of the Farm Street Jesuit Church, and is devoted to philosophy, theology, canon law and ecclesiastical history. A small amount of Latin American material has been acquired incidentally in pursuit of this collecting policy, and within the field of religion, there is a special current emphasis on problems of Church and State. Five current periodicals in the field are also taken.

Author and alphabetical subject catalogues. LC classification. Open access.

Hrs: Mon–Fri 0900–2100 (vacations 0930–1300, 1400–1600). Sat 0900–1230 (term only). Closed bank holidays and month of August.
Admission: At librarian's discretion (written recommendation).
Enquiries: By post and telephone.
Microreading: Microfiche and microfilm.
Copying: Xerox.
Lending: Through inter-library loan.
Union Record: BUCOP.

72 *Hispanic and Luso-Brazilian Council*

Canning House Library
2 Belgrave Square, London SWIX 8PJ
Tel: 01–235 2303/7
Librarian: G. H. Green BA

Dating from 1947, Canning House is the only library in the country devoted specifically to the cultures of the Spanish and Portuguese world, in Europe, Africa and Asia as well as

Latin America. It is supported by the contributions of firms which have an interest in these areas, and has also been helped from time to time by foundation money. Much of the material it acquires derives from the close contacts between the Council and the London embassies of the various Iberian and Latin American countries. The collection shows some bias towards modern aspects of Latin America, but it does contain material across the whole spectrum of Latin American studies, although its holdings are somewhat uneven in depth and strength. Total bookstock is 55,000; periodical titles exceed 400. The collection also includes maps and sheet music and a reference collection of Portuguese and Spanish technical dictionaries, whilst the Council Education Department is strong in audio-visual material (films, slides, discs). Regular exhibitions of Latin American artists are another feature of the library.

Author and classified subject catalogues. LC classification. Open access.

Hrs: Mon–Fri 0930–1300, 1400–1730. Closed bank holidays.
Admission: At librarian's discretion (letter of recommendation).
Enquiries: Preferably by telephone.
Lending: To users and through inter-library loan.
Union Record: BLLD, BUCOP, BUCLA, COLAESS.
PUBLICATIONS:
Catalogue, Boston, Mass., G. K. Hall, 1967, 5 vols (Luso-Brazilian supplement in preparation).
British bulletin of publications on Latin America, the West Indies, Portugal and Spain, 1949– (semi-annual, Apr and Oct).
Catalogue of Spanish and Portuguese dictionaries.

73 *House of Commons Library*

Palace of Westminster, Parliament Square, London SW1A 0AA
Tel: 01–219 3666/7
Librarian: D. C. L. Holland MA

The House of Commons Library dates from 1818, and aims to provide Members of Parliament 'with information rapidly on any of the multifarious matters which come before the House or to which their attentions are drawn by their parliamentary duties'. It has a good general collection of books and pamphlets, extensive holdings of British Parliamentary Papers (comprehensive) and of domestic and international official publications, and incomplete holdings of Commonwealth and colonial legislation.

Author and subject catalogues. Own classification. Open access for Parliamentarians only.

Hrs: For Members of Parliament and (by courtesy of Mr Speaker) for peers: at all hours when the House is sitting. Recess periods: 1000–1700.

For others: Mon–Fri 1000–1600 when House not sitting.

Admission: Bona fide researchers at librarian's discretion (prior appointment).

Enquiries: By post and (exceptionally) telephone.

Copying: Xerox (strictly limited).

Lending: To Members of House of Commons.

PUBLICATIONS:

The Library of the House of Commons handbook, 1970.

House of Commons Library Documents, 1–, London, HMSO, 1955– (occasional series, nine published to date).

74   *House of Lords Library*

Palace of Westminster, Parliament Square, London SW1A 0PW

Tel: 01–219 5242

Librarian: C. S. A. Dobson BA, FSA

The House of Lords Library, which dates from 1826, consists of a large collection of legal and parliamentary material, supplemented by a considerable amount of general literature (English and French history, biography, literature, heraldry, genealogy and English topography). Of immediate relevance to this directory are its extensive (but incomplete) holdings of colonial and Commonwealth acts and ordinances, including those affecting the West Indies.

Author catalogue, with special treatment for legal material. Own classification. Open access for Parliamentarians only.

Hrs: For Members of both Houses: at any time. For others: Mon–Fri 1000–1630 when House not sitting.

Admission: Bona fide researchers at librarian's discretion.

Enquiries: By post and (very exceptionally) telephone.

Copying: Xerox.

Lending: To peers (general literature only) and (for Members) to House of Commons Library.

PUBLICATIONS:

A short guide, 1972.

The library of the House of Lords: a short history, London, HMSO, 1972.

75   *Institute of Advanced Legal Studies Library, University of London*

25 Russell Square, London WC1B 5DR

Tel: 01–580 4868

Librarian: W. A. F. P. Steiner LLM, MA, ALA

The library began collecting in the field in 1948. Though it has given the area much greater priority since 1966, the collection of about 950 volumes and 64 periodical titles still constitutes only a minor part of the Institute's library. The collection of law reports includes 11 from the British West Indies and 11 from the rest of Latin America. Legislation is also well covered for the British West Indies but less consistently for the other countries of Latin America, the greatest strength being in Argentine and Brazilian material. Special emphasis is given to the acquisition of primary legal materials (legislation and law reports) and periodicals.

Author and alphabetical subject catalogues. Own classification. Closed access.

Hrs: Mon–Thur 1000–2000. Fri 1000–1730. Sat 1000–1230. Closed bank holidays and the second fortnight in September.

Admission: Academic teachers and postgraduate students of law; also certain persons holding a legal qualification, at the Director's discretion (written recommendation and fee may be required).

Enquiries: By post and telephone.

Copying: Xerox.

Lending: Through inter-library loan.

Union Record: BUCOP, BUCLA, Union list of legal periodicals, Union list of Commonwealth and South African law.

PUBLICATIONS:
Union list of legal periodicals: a location guide to holdings of legal periodicals in libraries in the United Kingdom, 3rd edn, 1968.
Union list of Commonwealth and South African law. A location guide to Commonwealth and South African legislation, law reports and digests held by libraries in the United Kingdom at May 1963.
Index to foreign legal periodicals, 1960–.

76 Institute of Archaeology Library, University of London

31–34 Gordon Square, London WC1H 0PY
Tel: 01–387 6052
Librarian: Miss G. C. Talbot MA, ALA
Subject enquiries to: Miss H. Bell BA (Assistant Librarian)

The library began collecting in this field in 1966. It now has 1050 volumes (including series) on Latin America which are shelved separately from the rest of the collection, and constitute one of a number of areas of interest for the library. Forty-five periodical titles are taken, and there is a small collection of material in microform. The Institute acquires from a wide range of sources, commercial dealers and exchange agreements both being used. There is also a small amount of associated relevant material on anthropology and folklore.

Author and alphabetical subject catalogues. LC classification. Open access.

Hrs: Mon–Fri 1000–2100 (vacations –1730). Sat 1000–1700 (except summer vacation). Closed bank holidays, one week at Christmas, 10 days at Easter, one week after Late Summer bank holiday, and one week at end of summer term.
Admission: At librarian's discretion (written recommendation and deposit).
Enquiries: By telephone.
Microreading: Microfilm.
Copying: Xerox.
Lending: To members and through inter-library loan.
Union Record: BUCLA.

77 Institute of Commonwealth Studies Library, University of London

27 Russell Square, London WC1B 5DS
Tel: 01–580 5876 extn 33
Librarian: Mrs P. M. Larby FLA

The library has been collecting material on the Commonwealth and French speaking areas of the Caribbean since it was founded in 1949. The collection constitutes one of a number of fields of special interest. No figures are available about the size of this part of the collection but 91 periodicals are currently received, not all of which are filed permanently. The main subject fields of interest are politics, economics, sociology and history, with some political party documents being held. Most of the material being acquired by the library is current, and there is a small number of exchange arrangements in operation.

Author and alphabetical subject catalogues. LC classification. Open access.

Hrs: Mon–Wed 0930–1900. Thur–Fri 0930–1800. Vacations: Mon–Fri 0930–1730. Closed bank holidays and one week at Christmas.
Admission: Post-graduate researchers.
Enquiries: By post and telephone.
Microreading: Microfilm.
Copying: Microfilm and Xerox.
Lending: Through inter-library loan.
Union Record: BUCOP, BUCLA, COLAESS.
PUBLICATIONS:
Guide to the library.
Accessions list (quarterly).
Theses in progress in Commonwealth Studies (annual).
List of current periodicals, 1970.

78 Institute of Contemporary History and Wiener Library

4 Devonshire Street, London W1N 2BH
Tel: 01–636 7247
Director: W. Laqueur

Founded in Amsterdam in 1933, the library has been established in London since 1939, and now contains about 60,000
volumes. Principal themes of the collection are German
history since 1914 (especially the history of the Third Reich),
and the recent history of Jewry and anti-Semitism. The library
has a small collection on Nazi influence in Latin America, and
on anti-Semitism there, mostly consisting of contemporary
source material. Some of the pamphlet material held is undoubtedly very rare. There is also an extensive classified
collection of press cuttings on these topics, some of them taken
from Latin American newspapers. Argentina is particularly
well represented in the press cuttings collection.

Author and classified subject catalogues. Own classification.
Partially open access.

Hrs: Mon–Fri 1000–1730. Closed bank holidays and three
weeks in late Summer.
Admission: Bona fide researchers (fee may be charged).
Enquiries: By post and telephone.
Microreading: Microfilm.
Copying: Microfilm.
Lending: To members and through inter-library loan.
Union Record: BLLD.
PUBLICATIONS:
Wiener Library Bulletin (quarterly).
Wiener Library Catalogue Series.

79   *Institute of Education, University of London*
Comparative Education Library
11–13 Ridgmount Street, London WC1E 7AH
Tel: 01–637 0846
Librarian: D. J. Foskett MA, FLA
Subject enquiries to: Mrs T. Bristow FLA (Comparative Education
Librarian)

The Comparative Education Library has 450 volumes and 53
periodical titles relating to Latin America arranged by country.
The Institute attempts to acquire all material concerned with
education and background material when this seems relevant.
Copies of Library of Congress proof slips provided by the

Institute of Latin American Studies are one of the sources of information about desirable material, and the Institute also uses other general bibliographical sources, and journal reviews. Perhaps a third of the material added to the collection is non-current. The collection also contains a small amount of micro-fiche material, which it is proposed to increase in the future.

Author, title and alphabetical subject catalogues. Own classi-fication. Open access.

Hrs: Mon–Thur 0930–2100. Fri 0930–1930. Sat 0930–1230. Vacations: Mon–Fri 0930–1930 (Aug –1700). Closed bank holidays and certain days adjoining.

Admission: Open to general public.

Enquiries: By post and telephone.

Microreading: Microfiche and microfilm.

Copying: Xerox.

Lending: To members and through inter-library loan.

Union Record: BLLD, BUCOP, BUCLA, LASER, COLAESS, Institutes of Education union list of periodicals.

PUBLICATIONS:

Catalogue of the library, Boston, Mass., G. K. Hall, 1972.

80   *Institute of Historical Research Library, University of London*

Senate House, London WC1E 7HU

Tel: 01–636 0272

Secretary and Librarian: W. Kellaway MA, FLA, FRHISTS, FSA

The library has been collecting in the Latin American field since about 1922, and now has substantially more than 5,000 volumes. They form a part of the Institute's library of some 90,000 volumes but are shelved in a separate room. According to an arrangement with University College Library (no. 108), the Institute specialises in primary materials, leaving the acquisition of secondary materials to the college. The combined resources of the two collections must be second to none in the field of history in the United Kingdom. The collection consists mainly of bibliographies, guides to manuscripts and archives, and collections of printed source materials, among which the following sets are particularly noteworthy: *Colección de docu-*

mentos . . . del real archivo de Indias (40 vols), *Documentos historicos* from the Biblioteca Nacional do Brasil (110 vols), *Publicações* of the Arquivo Nacional do Brasil (28 vols), *Documentos para la historia argentina* (22 vols), *Colección documental de la independencia del Perú* (30 vols), *Biblioteca de la Academia Nacional de la Historia de Venezuela* (more than 85 vols, in progress), and *Biblioteca de Historia Nacional Colombiana* (more than 110 vols, in progress). There are also collections of biographical dictionaries, and reference works, and more than 30 current periodicals. Special use is made of exchange, material being acquired in return for the *Bulletin of the Institute of Historical Research*. The Institute also receives a copy of each higher degree thesis presented to the University in the field of history.

Author catalogue. Own classification. Open access.

Hrs: Mon–Fri 0900–2100 (Aug –1900). Sat 0900–1700. Closed bank holidays.

Admission: Usually limited to honours graduates researching in history.

Enquiries: By post and (to members only) telephone.

Microreading: Microfilm.

Copying: Microfilm (for members only) and Xerox.

Typewriters: Permitted.

Lending: None.

Union Record: BUCOP, BUCLA.

81   *Institute of Latin American Studies Library, University of London*

31 Tavistock Square, London WC1H 9HA
Tel: 01–387 5671/2
Bibliographer/Librarian: Mrs B. M. Harrington BA, DIPLIB, ALA

Founded in 1965, following the University of London's decision to accept the invitation of the University Grants Committee to found a Parry Centre, the Institute's library has been limited as a matter of university policy to bibliographies, guides, directories and similar tools of reference. About a thousand volumes are held. There is also a small collection of monograph material, which consists of the works most in demand by students for the Master's degree in Latin American area studies, a small number of representative periodicals, most received in exchange for the *Journal of Latin American Studies*, and a few recent news sources (though not daily newspapers). The Institute houses the union catalogue of Latin American library materials, which records the holdings of some 60 libraries in an author file containing about 90,000 works relating to Latin America, and the West Indies.

Author, classified subject and geographical catalogues. Dewey classification (modified). Open access.

Hrs: Mon–Fri 0930–1730. Closed bank holidays and certain days adjoining.

Admission: At librarian's discretion.

Enquiries: By post and telephone.

Microreading: Microcard, microfiche and microfilm.

Copying: Xerox.

Typewriters: Permitted.

Lending: None.

Union Record: BUCLA.

INSTITUTE PUBLICATIONS:

New Latin American titles (termly list of additions to the union catalogue).

Latin American periodicals, 1970.

Latin American studies in the universities of the United Kingdom (annual).

Latin American monographs series (published for the Institute by the Athlone Press).

Staff research in progress or recently completed in the humanities and social sciences (annual).

Theses in Latin American studies at British universities in progress and completed (annual).

Postgraduate and research awards available in the field of Latin American studies, 1972.

P. Walne, *A guide to manuscript sources for the history of Latin America and the Caribbean in the British Isles*, London, Oxford University Press in collaboration with the Institute of Latin American Studies, University of London, 1973.

82 *International Book Information Services, Research Department*

New Building, North Circular Road, Neasden, London NW10 0JG

Tel: 01–459 7221

Telex: 261721 BOOKENTER LDN

Research executive with responsibility for Latin America: Ms J. Dutt

This is a commercial organisation set up by certain United Kingdom educational publishers. Formerly known as University Mailing Services, it exists to provide its clients with market research aids including worldwide mailing lists of institutions, libraries and individuals in higher education. For this purpose it maintains a library of university and college handbooks, directories and educational and trade journals. Its practice is to retain only the earliest and latest copies received of each handbook or directory. Interest in Latin America dates from 1968 and about 200 books are held on the area.

Classified subject catalogue. Own classification.

Hrs: Mon–Fri 0900–1700. Closed bank holidays.

Admission: Limited to employees of the company.

Enquiries: While IBIS has expressed readiness to answer occasional straightforward enquiries (preferably by telephone), enquirers (other than potential clients) should regard its library strictly as a last resort within its speciality.

Copying: Xerox.

Lending: None.

83 *International Coffee Organization (ICO) Library*

22 Berners Street, London W1P 4DD

Tel: 01–580 8591, 01–580 4208 and 01–637 3211

Research Officer: C. P. R. Dubois MA

The International Coffee Organization and its library were founded in 1962, the year the International Coffee Agreement was first signed. It contains 4,500 volumes excluding ICO documents and 400 current periodicals, of which more than 100 relate directly to Latin America and the West Indies. The main emphasis of the collection is on economic aspects of the production, marketing and consumption of coffee, but material is also held on technical aspects of coffee production, on the economies of coffee-producing countries, and on general questions of economic development and foreign trade. Some publications of such international bodies as the Organization of American States, the Economic Commission for Latin America, the United Nations Conference on Trade and Development, and the Food and Agriculture Organization are taken. A small but important historical collection relates to international coffee co-operation prior to the signing of the 1962 agreement.

Author and regional subject catalogues. Own classification (recent material on optical coincidence feature cards retrieval system). Open access.

Hrs: Mon–Fri 0930–1730. Closed bank holidays.

Admission: Bona fide graduate researchers at the discretion of the Executive Director (prior written application).

Enquiries: To members only by post and telephone.

Copying: Xerox.

Lending: Exceptionally through inter-library loan.

PUBLICATIONS:

List of periodical publications.

Accessions bulletin (monthly).

84   *International Cooperative Alliance Library*

11 Upper Grosvenor Street, London WIX 9PA

Tel: 01–499 5991

Librarian: Miss A. Lamming

The library has about 12,000 books and pamphlets on the world cooperative movement and such allied subjects as consumer affairs, education, economics, management and organisation. Holdings relevant to Latin America amount to some 300 books and 50 periodical titles, derived both from purchase and from exchange agreements with member organisations in the region. Very little of this relates to the English-speaking Caribbean.

Author and classified subject catalogues. Dewey classification. Open access.

Hrs: Mon–Fri 0845–1645. Closed bank holidays.

Admission: At librarian's discretion (prior application).
Enquiries: By post and telephone.
Copying: Xerox.
Typewriters: Permitted.
Lending: Through inter-library loan.

85 *King's College London Library, University of London*

Strand, London wc2r 2ls
Tel: 01–836 5454
Librarian:
Subject enquiries to: J. Callard ba (Assistant Librarian, extn 2132)

The college library of over 300,000 volumes, which was founded in 1831, includes a growing special collection of about 4,000 volumes on Latin American literature, begun in the early 1960s. It is shelved with the Spanish and Portuguese materials in the Modern Languages Library. Twenty periodicals are also taken in the field. The acquisitions programme makes use of Library of Congress proof slips provided by the University of London Institute of Latin American Studies. The library also contains material on colonial and modern history, especially relating to Portugal, some travel works on Latin America, and some basic bibliographical material.

Author and classified subject catalogues. LC classification. Open access.

Hrs: Mon–Fri 0930–2045 (summer vacation –1630. Other vacations –1745). Sat 0930–1245 (summer vacation closed. Other vacations –1200). Closed bank holidays, one week at Christmas and one week at Easter.
Admission: At librarian's discretion (written application).
Microreading: Microcard and microfilm.
Copying: Xerox.
Lending: To members and through inter-library loan.
Union Record: BUCOP, BUCLA.
PUBLICATIONS:
Guide to library facilities.

86   *Lloyds Bank International Limited*

Economics Department Library
100 Pall Mall, London SW1Y 5HP
Tel: 01–930 0831 extn 89
Librarian: Mrs M. T. Fletcher BA, ALAA

The library has been acquiring Latin American material since its creation by the then Bank of London and South America in the 1920s, and the bank's overseas branches are a primary source of its acquisitions. The book collection is small, but some 600 periodicals and annual reports are received that originate from, or deal with, Latin America. The library is particularly strong in the publications of Latin American central banks. A notable feature of the library is its extensive collection of press cuttings from Latin America whose compilation began in the 1920s.

Author, title and classified subject catalogues. Own classification. Open access.

Hrs: Mon–Fri 0915–1700. Closed bank holidays.
Admission: At librarian's discretion (prior written application).
Enquiries: By post and telephone.
Copying: Xerox (by special arrangement).
Lending: To the Bank's employees, and through inter-library loan.
Union Record: COLAESS (as Bank of London and South America Ltd).

87   *London Borough of Hackney Library Services*

Central Library
Mare Street, Hackney, London E8 1HG
Tel: 01–985 8262
Borough Librarian: C. J. Long FLA

Homerton Branch Library
Brooksby's Walk, Homerton, London E9 6DF
Tel: 01–985 8262 extn 33
Branch Librarian: F. May

Under a subject specialisation scheme begun by the then

metropolitan libraries in 1946, which became fully effective from about 1948 and was later extended by amalgamation to cover all public libraries in South East England, Hackney public library authority accepted responsibility for buying all British current publications on Latin American history, geography and travel. Other member libraries were to pass any older material in this field to Hackney as they withdrew it from stock. From 1953, this responsibility has been interpreted to imply all works classified into those subjects in the *British National Bibliography*. The collection now consists of 1,900 volumes (almost all in English) and 8 periodical titles. Whilst the bulk of the collection is stored, for administrative convenience, at Homerton Branch Library, books in current demand are kept in the stock of the Mare Street Central Library.

Author and alphabetical subject catalogues. Dewey classification. Open access.

Hrs: Mon–Tues, Thur–Fri 0900–2000. Sat 0900–1700. Closed bank holidays.

Admission: Open to general public.

Enquiries: By post and telephone.

Microreading: Microfilm.

Copying: Xerox.

Lending: To users (readers' tickets from other U.K. public libraries accepted) and through inter-library loan.

Union Record: BUCOP, LASER, COLAESS.

88   *London Borough of Tower Hamlets Libraries*

Central Library (administrative headquarters)
277 Bancroft Road, Stepney, London E1 4DQ
Tel: 01–980 4366
Bethnal Green Area Library (French and German literature collection)
Cambridge Heath Road, Bethnal Green, London E2 0HL
Tel: 01–980 3902
Borough Librarian: H. Ward FLA
Subject enquiries to: Mrs M. M. Veneer BA, ALA (Senior Assistant responsible for French and German literature collection. *Tel:* 01–980 3902)

Tower Hamlets has responsibility under the Inner London
Subject Specialisation Scheme for literature in Portuguese. Its
present holdings are housed in the French and German literature room at Bethnal Green Area Library, and include about
200 works by Brazilian authors or with Brazilian imprints.
Accessions are by purchase and the transfer of withdrawn stock
from other London boroughs. No periodicals are taken.

Author and classified subject catalogues. Dewey classification. Open access.

Hrs: Mon–Fri 0900–2000. Sat 0900–1700. Closed bank holidays.
Admission: Open to general public.
Enquiries: By post and telephone.
Copying: Xerox.
Lending: To users (readers' tickets from other U.K. public
libraries accepted) and through inter-library loan.
Union Record: BLLD, LASER.
PUBLICATIONS:
Books in Portuguese [a stock list].
French & German literature [a leaflet about the collection].

89   *London Library*

14 St James's Square, London SW1Y 4LG
Tel: 01–930 7705
Librarian: S. Gillam BLITT, MA

The library has collected in this field since its foundation in
1841, and, though it is impossible to give an accurate estimate
of the size of the collection, which is not kept separate, it must
now amount to several thousand volumes in the fields of literature, history, biography, travel and topography. There are
also about a dozen periodicals, most of them old.

Author and alphabetical subject catalogues. Own classification. Open access.

Hrs: Mon–Sat 0930–1730 (Thur –1930). Closed bank holidays.
Admission: At Committee's discretion (prior application and
fee required).
Enquiries: By post and telephone.
Copying: Xerox (members only).
Lending: To members and through inter-library loan.

PUBLICATIONS:

Catalogue of the London Library. 1913–14, (2 vols). *Supplement 1913–20*, 1920. *Supplement 1920–28*, 1929. *Third supplement 1928–50*, 1953.
Subject-index of the London Library, 1909. *Volume II. Additions 1909–22*, 1923. *Volume III. Additions 1923–38*, 1938. *Volume IV. Additions 1938–53*, 1955.

90 London School of Economics and Political Science, University of London

British Library of Political and Economic Science
Houghton Street, London WC2A 2AE
Tel: 01–405 7686
Librarian: D. A. Clarke MA
Subject enquiries to: Miss J. V. Garlant MA (Assistant Librarian in charge of Latin American materials, extn 347)

The Latin American material in the British Library of Political and Economic Science is found both in the open shelf collection, and in the unclassified closed access stacks. It is therefore impossible to say how many volumes are held but more than 15,000 have been added since the late 1950s. Right from the library's foundation in 1896, the area was one of those in which the library showed an interest, and the collecting policy has been expanded as the knowledge of sources of publications increased and funds became available. The collection is particularly strong in the School's traditional subjects of interest, that is politics, economics and sociology, and any area limitations on the collection have arisen through restrictions on the availability of material rather than as a matter of policy. In addition to the above mentioned interests, the library now collects especially in the following fields: constitutional, criminal and labour law (but not works about law), social anthropology, and the history (especially the economic history) of the national period. Non-current as well as current material is being added to the collection, and special acquisitions procedures include exchange agreements regarding serials with research institutes and university departments, exchanges of official duplicates with government libraries, and a blanket order for the official publications of Uruguay and Paraguay. The library is a deposit library for the publications of the United Nations and its agencies, and for the publications of certain other international bodies such as the Organization of American States.

Author and classified subject catalogues. LC classification (much closed access material unclassified). Partial open access.

Hrs: Mon–Fri 1000–2120 (August –1700). Sat 1000–1700 (except July, August). Closed bank holidays, one week at Easter and one week at Christmas.

Admission: At librarian's discretion. For protracted research, application form, and letter of recommendation required.

Enquiries: By post and telephone.

Microreading: Microcard, microfiche and microfilm.

Copying: Xerox.

Typewriters: Permitted.

Lending: To members and through inter-library loan.

Union Record: BLLD, BUCOP, BUCLA, COLAESS.

PUBLICATIONS:

Notes for readers.

Outline of the resources of the library.

Monthly list of accessions.

London bibliography of the social sciences, 1931–.

91 *London School of Hygiene and Tropical Medicine Library, University of London*

Keppel Street, Gower Street, London WCIE 7HT
Tel: 01–636 8636 extn 276
Librarian: V. J. Glanville ALA

The library began collecting in the field in about 1930, and the collection which has not been kept separate, constitutes a minor part of the library. It consists of about 1,000 books, 5,000 volumes of periodicals and 300 volumes of official reports. The library seeks to acquire all medical, vital statistical, and biological literature in the field of preventive medicine, the greater proportion of the acquisitions being current material. Some material is acquired by exchange. The library occasionally acquires non-book materials where relevant.

Author and alphabetical subject catalogues. Barnard classification. Open access.

Hrs: Mon–Fri 0930–2000 (vacations –1700). Sat 0930–1200 (except Aug and preceding a bank holiday Mon). Closed bank holidays.
Admission: Open to general public.
Enquiries: By post and (to members only) telephone.
Microreading: Microcard, microfiche and microfilm.
Copying: Xerox.
Lending: To members, and through inter-library loan.
Union Record: BLLD, BUCOP, BUCLA, WLSP.
PUBLICATIONS:
Dictionary-Catalogue of the London School of Hygiene and Tropical Medicine, University of London, Boston, Mass., G. K. Hall, 1967. *First supplement,* Boston, Mass., G. K. Hall, 1971.

92   *Ministry of Defence (Central and Army) Library*

Old War Office Building, Whitehall, London SW1A 2EU
Tel: 01–930 9400
Chief Librarian: D. W. King OBE, FLA (extn 0015)

The library, which now administers the library of the Royal United Services Institution, has a total stock of about 500,000 books and pamphlets, and 1,100 current periodicals, and includes some material of naval and air interest. The Latin American material relates both to the military history of the area and the current strategic situation and the background to it. The historical collection has material both on the struggle for independence in the early nineteenth century, and on the wars between the newly independent states. The memoirs of British soldiers who campaigned officially or unofficially in Latin America are a feature of the historical collection.

Author and alphabetical subject catalogues. UDC classification. Open access.

Hrs: Mon–Fri 0900–1730. Closed bank holidays.
Admission: Bona fide researchers.
Enquiries: By post and telephone.
Microreading: Microfiche and microfilm.

Copying: Xerox and reader/printer.
Lending: To users and through inter-library loan.
Union Record: BLLD.
PUBLICATIONS:
Accessions (also covers the Naval and Air libraries) (Six-weekly).
Selected accessions (subject lists) (weekly).
Recent military books.
Periodical list.
Periodical articles of defence interest (weekly).
Subject lists.
Printed index to subject lists (annual).

93   *Ministry of Defence (Navy)*

Naval Historical Library
Empress State Building, Lillie Road, London sw6 1TR
Tel: 01–385 1244 extn 3246
Librarian: Lieutenant-Commander P. K. Kemp OBE

The total stock of over 160,000 volumes and 100,000 pamphlets is devoted to maritime history and especially the history of the British navy and its personnel, to shipbuilding and naval science, and to voyages and travels in general. In a rich collection of early voyages, there is a number of travel accounts relating to Latin America in the first half of the nineteenth century. Material on naval campaigns and actions (including the Latin American theatre), hydrographical surveys, strategy, tactics, seamanship, navigation and shipbuilding are other aspects of the collection. The charts and maps date back mainly to the first half of the nineteenth century, but there are several eighteenth-century items and a few from the seventeenth century.

Author and classified subject catalogues. Own classification. Open access.

Hrs: Mon–Fri 1000–1700. Closed bank holidays.
Admission: Bona fide researchers.
Enquiries: By post and telephone.
Lending: To other government departments.

94 *National Maritime Museum Library*

Romney Road, Greenwich, London SE10 9NF

Tel: 01–858 4422 extn 265

Librarian: M. W. B. Sanderson MA, PHD

Founded in 1934, the library of the National Maritime Museum has a total collection of some 50,000 books, 100,000 pamphlets, and 80 periodicals on all aspects of seafaring, naval, merchant and recreational. The main interest is in British maritime history, which is itself important for its West Indian connections, but material from and about other countries is also collected. Particularly relevant are the collections on Navigation, Voyages and Travel, and Piracy, and that of Atlases. There is further material of interest in naval history, biography, topography, merchant shipping, naval architecture, and fisheries. There are films in the Education Department, slides in the Department of Pictures and tape recordings in the Department of Manuscripts.

Author and classified subject catalogues. Own classification. Closed access.

Hrs: Mon–Fri (and, by prior appointment only, Sat) 1000–1300, 1400–1700. Closed bank holidays and third week in February.

Admission: At Director's discretion (application form and written recommendation).

Enquiries: To ticket holders, preferably by post.

Microreading: Microfilm.

Copying: Microfilm and Xerox.

Lending: None.

PUBLICATIONS:

Catalogue of the library, London, HMSO, 1968– (volumes on voyages and travel, biography, atlases and cartography, and piracy already published).

95 *Overseas Development Institute Library*

10–11 Percy Street, London W1P 0JB

Tel: 01–637 3622

Librarian: Mrs L. Lowenthal

The library which dates from 1960 possesses some 8,000 volumes and 200 current periodicals dealing with all aspects of aid and development in the Third World. It is not known what proportion of this relates to Latin America and the West Indies. The subject section covers general economics of development, finance, foreign trade, agriculture, population problems, the institutional and sociological aspects of development, theoretical studies on aid, and evaluations. The regional section contains economic material on specific regions and countries with special emphasis on economic surveys and development plans. A third section is concerned with the aid programmes of donor countries and organisations. The reference section contains, apart from general reference books, directories and reports of organisations active in the field of aid and development, conference papers, international statistics and bibliographies. Files of newspaper cuttings, press releases, references to periodical articles and similar material, arranged according to subject and/or region, have been kept since 1963.

Author and classified subject catalogues. Own classification. Open access.

Hrs: Mon–Fri 1000–1800. Closed bank holidays.
Admission: At librarian's discretion.
Enquiries: By telephone.
Lending: None.
PUBLICATIONS:
Periodical review (monthly index to periodicals taken).

96   *Queen Mary College Library, University of London*

Mile End Road, London E1 4NS
Tel: 01–980 4811
Librarian: T. H. Bowyer BSC(ECON), FLA

The library has been collecting in the field since about 1965 and now has some 1,500 volumes (mainly recent publications) and 15 current periodicals, predominantly devoted to literature and literary criticism.

Author and classified subject catalogues. LC classification. Open access.

Hrs: Mon–Fri 0915–2130 (vacations –1700). Sat 1000–1800

(term only). Closed bank holidays and a few days at Christmas and Easter.

Admission: At librarian's discretion (written application).
Enquiries: By post and telephone.
Microreading: Microcard, microfiche and microfilm.
Copying: Xerox.
Lending: To members and through inter-library loan.
Union Record: BLLD, BUCOP, BUCLA, LASER.

97   *Reuters Limited*

85 Fleet Street, London EC4
Tel: 01–353 6060 extn 227
Telex: 28354 ECONREUTER LDN
Librarian: E. Somjen BSC(ECON)

The collection, established 1944, consists almost entirely of teleprinter tapes arranged alphabetically by specific subjects, with a small number of books classified by Dewey. The library also maintains a list, revised daily, of the governments of all sovereign states.

Classified and alphabetical subject catalogues. Closed access.

Hrs: Mon–Fri open 24 hours. Sat 0800–2300. Sun 0900–2400.
Admission: At management's discretion (minimum charge £5).
Authorised visitors are normally restricted to office hours.
Enquiries: By post and telephone.
Copying: Xerox.
Typewriters: Permitted.
Lending: None.

98   *Royal Anthropological Institute of Great Britain and Ireland Library*

6 Burlington Gardens, London WIX 2EX
Tel: 01–734 6370
Librarian: Miss B. J. Kirkpatrick FLA

The Institute has been collecting in the Latin American field since 1843. Though it is not kept separate, and is of indeterminate size, the Latin American material forms a comparatively strong part of the Institute's collection. The library has 201 periodicals relevant to the field (not all of them current). Material in the Sir Richard Burton collection is a special feature, as is the collection of offprints of periodical articles. Almost all the journals are acquired by exchange.

Author and classified subject catalogues. Bliss classification (modified). Open access to members only.

Hrs: Mon–Fri 1000–1645. Closed bank holidays, one week at Christmas and part of August.
Admission: On the recommendation of a Fellow.
Enquiries: By post and telephone.
Copying: Xerox.
Lending: To members and through inter-library loan.
Union Record: BLLD, BUCOP, COLAESS.

PUBLICATIONS:
Anthropological index to current periodicals in the library of the RAI (quarterly).

99   *Royal Commonwealth Society Library*

18 Northumberland Avenue, London WC2N 5BJ
Tel: 01–930 6733
Librarian: D. H. Simpson FLA

The Library's total stock consists of over 400,000 volumes, pamphlets, official documents and serials. The scope of the collection is the Commonwealth and its members, past and present, and for these areas a wide range of subjects, including history, geography, politics, economics, literature, education, art, and natural history, is covered. The main arrangement of both catalogue and stock is geographical, and there is a very substantial section on the Caribbean, including printed material from the eighteenth century onwards and many official publications. A large collection of pamphlets on slavery contains much West Indian material. Articles in periodicals are catalogued. There is also material on the Falkland Islands, and a small collection on non-Commonwealth countries of Central and South America. The Library's photographic section includes West Indian material.

Author and classified subject catalogues. Own classification. Open access.

Hrs: Mon–Fri 1000–1900 (summer –1730). Sat 1000–1800 (summer –1730). Closed bank holidays.
Admission: At Librarian's discretion.
Enquiries: By post and telephone.
Microreading: Microfilm.
Copying: Xerox.
Lending: To members.
Union Record: BLLD.
PUBLICATIONS:
Subject catalogue, 4 vols, 1930–37 (repr. 1967).
Biography catalogue, 1961.
Subject catalogue (supplementing the preceding) 7 vols, Boston, Mass., G. K. Hall, 1971.
RES bibliographies.
Library notes.

100   *Royal Geographical Society Library*

Kensington Gore, London SW7 2AR
Tel: 01–589 5466
Librarian: G. S. Dugdale MA, FLA

The Latin American section of the library covers all aspects of the geography of Latin America, and has been growing since the foundation of the Society in 1830. It now comprises some 3,200 volumes, and about 100 periodicals (not all current). Since the library is arranged by country, the Latin American material is separately shelved. Early periodical runs, some beginning before 1900 (especially from Brazil), and material on boundary disputes (much of it official) are special features of interest. Material, mostly current, continues to be acquired intermittently, from Spain, Portugal and Latin America as well as from Britain and the United States. The *Geographical Journal* is a feature of exchange arrangements with appropriate Latin American geographical societies. The map room is administered separately from the library and is under the charge of the Keeper of the Map Room.

    Author and classified subject catalogues. Own classification. Open access.
Hrs: Mon–Fri 0930–1730. Closed bank holidays and three

weeks in summer, or such period as the Council of the Society may determine.

Admission: At the discretion of the Director and Secretary (prior written application; fee usually required).

Enquiries: By post and telephone.

Copying: Xerox.

Lending: To members and through inter-library loan.

Union Record: BLLD (partial), BUCOP, COLAESS, WLSP.

PUBLICATIONS:

New Geographical Literature and Maps (2 issues per annum).

G. R. Crone, 'The library of the Royal Geographical Society', *Geog. Journal*, 121, 1955, pp. 27–32.

Catalogue of the library of the R.G.S., 1895.

101   *Royal Institute of British Architects* (*RIBA*)

Sir Banister Fletcher Library
66 Portland Place, London WIN 4AD
Tel: 01–580 5533 extn 244
Librarian: D. E. Dean MA, DIPED, ALA

The RIBA Library, founded 1834, has some 100,000 books and pamphlets on all aspects of world architecture, past and present, and related subjects. Material of Latin American interest amounts to about 1,000 items and 16 periodical titles, with emphasis on Mexico (particularly Mayan architecture and other historical aspects), Brazil (especially Brasilia), Peru and Cuba.

Author, alphabetical subject and classified subject catalogues. UDC classification. Open access.

Hrs: Mon 1000–1700. Tue–Fri 1000–2000. Sat 1000–1330. Closed bank holidays and 4 weeks in August.

Admission: Open to general public.

Enquiries: By post and telephone.

Copying: Photocopier.

Lending (from the small loan collection): To members and through inter-library loan.

Union Record: BLLD (very small proportion of stock only), BUCOP.

PUBLICATIONS:
RIBA Library Bulletin, 1945–72.
RIBA Annual Review of Periodical Articles, 1965–72.
Architectural periodicals index, 1972– (replacing both of the foregoing).

102 *Royal Institute of International Affairs Library*

Chatham House, 10 St James's Square, London SW1Y 4LE
Tel: 01–930 2233
Librarian: Miss D. M. Hamerton MA, ALA
Press Librarian: Miss S. J. Boyde MA, DIPLIB

The Institute whose interest lies in the post 1918 period has been collecting in the field since its foundation in 1920, and the 2,000 books and 1,200 pamphlets on Latin America which it now holds form a part of its total collection of some 130,000 books and pamphlets. Forty-seven periodicals relating to Latin America are also currently taken, thirty of which originate in Latin America itself. The library is a depository for the publications of the United Nations and its agencies, such as the Economic Commission for Latin America, and in addition has a collection of official material from the Organization of American States, as well as statistical annuals and bank reports. A subject index to 200 selected periodicals in its field is maintained. The Press Library has maintained since 1924 an international archive of closely analysed and indexed cuttings taken from daily newspapers in Western European languages. All aspects of international affairs are covered including political and economic developments in Latin America. The Press Library also has custody of a collection of press cuttings made in the Foreign Office Research Department during the Second World War.

Author, alphabetical subject (for pre-1950 material) and classified subject (for post-1949 material) catalogues. Own classification. Open access.

Hrs: Mon–Fri 1000–1800 (Thur –1900). Sat 1000–1700 (June–September –1300). Closed bank holidays and certain days adjoining and throughout August.

Admission: At librarian's discretion (post-graduate research workers only).

Enquiries: By post, and (to members only) telephone.

Microreading: Microfilm.

Copying: Xerox.

Lending: To personal members, to member libraries and through inter-library loan.

Union Record: BLLD, BUCOP, BUCLA.

PUBLICATIONS:

Catalogue of Periodicals currently received in Chatham House library.

Index to Periodical Articles 1950–1964 in the Library of the Royal Institute of International Affairs, Boston, Mass., G. K. Hall, 1965. *Supplement 1965–72,* Boston, Mass., G. K. Hall, 1973.

103 *Royal Society of Medicine Library*

1 Wimpole Street, London WIM 8AE

Tel: 01–580 2070

Librarian: P. Wade BA, FLA

The library has been collecting material from Latin America since 1907. The material acquired has not been kept separate, is of indeterminate quantity and forms only a minor part of the Society's total collection. It consists predominantly of periodicals. Some journals are acquired by standing order, others by exchange against the *Proceedings of the Royal Society of Medicine.*

Author and alphabetical subject catalogues. UDC classification. Open access.

Hrs: Mon–Fri 0930–2130. Sat 0930–1730. Closed bank holidays.

Admission: On the recommendation of a Fellow.

Enquiries: By post and telephone to members only.

Microreading: Microfilm (members only).

Copying: Xerox.

Lending: To members only.

Union Record: BUCOP, COLAESS.

104 *School of Oriental and African Studies Library, University of London*

Malet Street, London WC1 7HP
Tel: 01–637 2388
Librarian: B. C. Bloomfield MA, FLA

Since about 1950, the library has been building up a special collection on Amerindian languages of North, Central and South America which now amounts to over 500 volumes. Up to half the material added is non-current or reprint material. The library has an agreement with the Centro Interamericano de Libros Académicos, by which it is notified of new relevant material.

Author, title, and classified subject catalogues. Dewey classification. Open access.

Hrs: Mon–Fri 0900–1900 (vacations –1730). Sat 0930–1230. Closed bank holidays.
Admission: At librarian's discretion (written application with two guarantors).
Enquiries: By post and telephone.
Microreading: Microfiche and microfilm.
Copying: Xerox.
Typewriters: Permitted.
Lending: To members and (exceptionally) to non-members (£5 deposit), and through inter-library loan.
Union Record: BUCOP, BUCLA.

PUBLICATIONS:
Library guide, 2nd edn, London, 1973.
Library catalogue, Boston, Mass., G. K. Hall, 1963. *Supplement*, Boston, Mass., G. K. Hall, 1968. *2nd Supplement*, Boston, Mass., G. K. Hall, 1974.

105 *Trades Union Congress Library*

Congress House, Great Russell Street, London WC1B 3LF
Tel: 01–636 4030 extn 238
Librarian: Miss C. Coates ALA

The library of the Trades Union Congress, which was founded in 1922, is devoted to labour, trade unionism and social, economic and working conditions throughout the world. Material on Latin America is largely derived from exchange agreements with trade union organisations in the region.

Author and alphabetical subject catalogues. LC classification. Open access.

Hrs: Mon–Fri 0930–1715. Closed bank holidays.
Admission: At librarian's discretion (prior application).
Enquiries: By post and telephone.
Lending: To members and (of duplicated items) to non-members and through inter-library loan.

106 *Tropical Products Institute Library*

56–62 Gray's Inn Road, London WC1X 8LU
Tel: 01–242 5412
Librarian: J. Wright ALA

Since about 1895, the library has been collecting material on the agriculture and the plant and animal products of former British colonies. The Latin American material constitutes only a minor part of the overall collection of 50,000 books and 100,000 pamphlets and is not kept separately, but it may amount to 10,000 items. There are also 1,000 current periodicals. Use is made of exchange agreements with major agricultural departments and institutions overseas.

Author and classified subject catalogues and technical subject index to relevant papers in the library's serial holdings since 1895. UDC classification (for books and pamphlets). Most heavily used material on open access.

Hrs: Mon–Fri 0900–1800. Closed bank holidays.
Admission: Open to general public.
Enquiries: By post and telephone.
Microreading: Microfiche.
Copying: Xerox.
Lending: To members and through inter-library loan.
Union Record: BUCOP.

107 *United Nations Information Centre*

14–15 Stratford Place, London W1N 9AF
Tel: 01–629 3816

Librarian: Miss M. A. McAfee

As one of 50 information centres throughout the world, the Centre Library holds the sales publications of the Economic Commission for Latin America (ECLA) and some of its mimeographed material. Earlier ECLA material in English is held in microform.

General United Nations catalogues and document indexes. Open access.

Hrs: Mon, Wed, Thur 1000–1700. Closed bank holidays and one week in August.

Admission: Open to general public.

Enquiries: By post and telephone.

Microreading: Microfilm.

Copying: Xerox.

Lending (current material only): To users and through inter-library loan.

108 *University College London Library, University of London*

Gower Street, London WC1E 6BT

Tel: 01–387 7050

Librarian: J. W. Scott BA, ALA

Subject enquiries to: (for anthropology) C. Marmoy FLA (extn 245); (for geography) Mrs R. Obelkovich BA (extn 242); (for history) M. Jahn BA, MPHIL (extn 243); (for literature) I. Martin MA (extn 241).

Founded in 1826, the college began the systematic collection of Latin American material in 1948, the year which saw the establishment of the Chair of Latin American History at the college, the first academic post specifically dedicated to Latin American studies in the United Kingdom. The library now holds over 10,000 items in the Latin American field. The most important collection relates to history, and contains 6,500 items of secondary material, primary material being collected by the Institute of Historical Research (no. 80). The combined holdings are second to none in this field in the United Kingdom. The history collection includes material on contemporary economic and social history, and on all parts of the area except the English-, French- and Dutch-speaking Caribbean.

Special emphasis is also given to geography (1,700 items), Spanish American literature (1,500 items) and anthropology (600 items). The geography collection is strongest on human and economic geography, including cultural and economic change, agriculture, migration and urbanisation, and sociology, with a regional emphasis on Mexico, Brazil, Venezuela, part of Argentina, Chile, Colombia and Peru. The literature collection consists mainly of modern fiction and poetry, with an emphasis on Argentine and Mexican writers. Mexico and Brazil are major interests of the anthropology collection. Some non-current material is acquired and there are exchange and donation agreements especially for bank reports and Argentine censuses. Over 300 periodicals are taken, most relating to geography. Whilst the Latin American history collection is housed in a special room, the other materials are incorporated with their respective subject collections.

Author and classified subject catalogues. Own classification. Open access.

Hrs: Mon–Fri 0930–2100 (Summer vacation –1700, other vacations –1900) Sat 0930–1230 (except Summer vacation). Closed bank holidays and one week at Christmas and one week at Easter.

Admission: At librarian's discretion (prior written application)
Enquiries: By post and telephone.
Microreading: Microfiche and microfilm.
Copying: Microfilm and Xerox.
Lending: To users and through inter-library loan.
Union Record: BUCOP, BUCLA, COLAESS.
PUBLICATIONS:
Library guide.

109   *University of London*

In 1965, the University of London accepted an invitation from the University Grants Committee (UGC) to establish a centre for Latin American studies as recommended in the report of the UGC's Committee on Latin American Studies (the 'Parry' report). An Institute of Latin American Studies (no. 81) was founded, and acts as a coordinating and bibliographical centre, both for the University of London, and in some respects for all centres of Latin American studies in the United Kingdom. It was decided by the university that existing developments at other schools and institutes of the university made it unnecessary to establish a further research collection at the newly founded Institute. Instead special funds for the strengthening of existing collections were distributed among schools and institutes of the university on the basis of their own reasoned submissions, and with responsibility for definite subject areas assigned to each as follows: University Library (bibliographies, maps, periodicals, music and general collection, no. 110), King's College (literature, no. 85), London School of Economics (economics, politics and sociology, no. 90), University College (history, geography, economics, colonial literature and anthropology, no. 108), Institute of Advanced Legal Studies (law, no. 75), Institute of Archaeology (archaeology, no. 76), and Institute of Historical Research (history source materials, no. 80). Funds have also been made available to the following schools and institutes for the strengthening of their library holdings in the fields specified: Bedford College (geography, no. 47), Institute of Education (education, no. 79), London School of Hygiene and Tropical Medicine (preventive medicine and public health, no. 91), Queen Mary College (literature, no. 96), School of Oriental and African Studies (Amerindian languages, no. 104), and Wye College (rural sociology, no. 4). Whilst the combined strength of the libraries of the university is second to none in this field in the United Kingdom, those seeking more information on these resources must consult the individual entries for the libraries mentioned.

110   *University of London Library*
Senate House, Malet Street, London WC1E 7HU
Tel: 01–636 4514
Director of Central Library Services and Goldsmiths' Librarian: K. Garside MA
Subject enquiries to: Miss P. Noble BA (Senior Assistant Librarian with responsibility for the Latin American collection)
Since 1968, the library has been intensively developing its

collection in this field, though it had already collected a good deal of material relating to the area before that time. The collection now amounts to about 8,000 volumes which are separately shelved. About 140 periodicals are also taken. The library has 880 maps and 26 atlases relevant to the area, and in addition to its music collection of about 100 books, a substantial number of scores and gramophone records. Bibliography is particularly well represented, both in the existing holdings and in the new acquisitions, though the collection also continues to develop on general lines. Little material published before 1955 is now being acquired; booksellers' catalogues are the main source of material, a few periodicals being acquired by exchange. The Goldsmiths' collection contains some early travel accounts of Latin America, and some material on economic conditions in the area before 1850.

Author and classified subject catalogues. Bliss classification. Open access.

Hrs: Mon–Fri 0930–2100 (Summer vacation –1730). Sat 0930–1730. Closed bank holidays and one day following except after Spring bank holiday.
Admission: At the Director's discretion (written application).
Enquiries: By post and telephone.
Microreading: Microcard, microfiche and microfilm.
Copying: Microfilm and Xerox.
Typewriters: Permitted (separate room).
Lending: To members and through inter-library loan.
Union Record: BLLD, BUCOP, BUCLA, COLAESS.
PUBLICATIONS:
Introductory guide.
Notes for new readers.

111   *Venezuelan Embassy/Embajada de los Estados Unidos de Venezuela*

Venezuelan Library
3 Hans Crescent, London SW1X OLX
Tel: 01–584 4206/7
Librarian: Mrs C. Pizani
The library is primarily for use by the Embassy staff. It has

about 1,800 books, mainly Venezuelan official publications. It is strong in international law, Venezuelan history and tourist material, but has very little literature.

No catalogues. Unclassified. Open access.

Hrs: Mon–Fri 0930–1300, 1430–1700. Closed 1 Jan, 19 Mar, 19 Apr, Maundy Thur, Good Fri, 1 May, 24 Jun, 5 Jul, 12 Oct, 17 and 25 Dec.

Admission: Open to general public.

Enquiries: By post and telephone.

Lending: At librarian's discretion to users, and through inter-library loan.

112   Victoria and Albert Museum Library

Cromwell Road, London sw7
Tel: 01–589 6371
Keeper of the Library: J. P. Harthan MA, FLA

The total stock of the library is over 400,000 books and covers all branches of the fine and applied arts. Some of the material relates to Latin America. Current exchanges are maintained with institutions in Latin America which publish relevant material.

Author and alphabetical subject catalogues. Own classification. Closed access.

Hrs: Mon–Sat 1000–1750. Closed bank holidays.

Admission: Bona fide researchers. Tickets required by regular readers.

Enquiries: By post and telephone.

Microreading: Microfilm.

Copying: Xerox.

Lending: None.

PUBLICATIONS:
Accessions list.

113   Wellcome Institute of the History of Medicine

Wellcome Historical Medical Library
Wellcome Building, 183 Euston Road, London NW1 2BP
Tel: 01–387 4477

Librarian: E. Gaskell BA, ALA

Subject enquiries to: R. Price MA, ALA (Assistant Librarian in charge of the Latin American collection, extn 166)

The library has been collecting in the field of the history of Latin American medicine since 1890, and now has a special room devoted to the Latin American collection. As well as 65 periodical titles, the collection contains some 6,200 volumes, a total which includes the León collection of nineteenth-century reprints, theses and pamphlets from Mexico, ethnological and travel works, and Mexican theses (1860–1950). Additional material to be added to this total includes the collection on the American Indian tribes and their medicine, the medicine and culture of the primitive American civilisations (Aztec, Maya and Inca), reproductions of their illuminated codices, 134 catalogued manuscripts of American medical interest (largely of the colonial period) and many uncounted reprints, pamphlets, booksellers' and auction-house catalogues, and some transparencies. Special features of the library are an almost complete collection of medical *Mexicana* to 1833, and a fairly complete collection for the remainder of Latin America and the West Indies during the colonial period, including colonial newspapers and facsimiles of works not otherwise available.

Author and alphabetical subject catalogues. Barnard classification (Latin American material not classified). Closed access.

Hrs: Mon–Sat 1000–1700. Closed bank holidays.
Admission: Open to general public.
Enquiries: By post and telephone.
Microreading: Microfiche and microfilm.
Copying: Microfilm and Xerox.
Lending: Exceptionally through inter-library loan.
Union Record: BUCLA.

PUBLICATIONS:

A catalogue of printed books in the Wellcome Historical Medical Library, Volume I: Books printed before 1641, 1962. *Volume II: Books printed between 1641 and 1850; A–E,* 1966. *Volume III: Books printed between 1641 and 1850; F–L,* (in press).

S. A. J. Moorat, *Catalogue of Western manuscripts on medicine and science in the Wellcome Historical Medical Library, Volume I:*

Mss. written before A.D. 1650, 1962. *Volume II: MSS. Written after A.D. 1650* (2 pts), 1973.
Current work in the history of medicine. An international bibliography, 1954– (quarterly).

114 *Westfield College, University of London*

Caroline Skeel Library
Kidderpore Avenue, Hampstead, London NW3 7ST
Tel: 01–435 7141 extn 308
Librarian: Miss D. M. Moore BA, FLA
The library has been collecting in the field since about 1966 and has up to 1,500 volumes, and 12 periodical titles, with no special emphases.
Author and classified subject catalogues. LC classification. Open access.
Hrs: Mon–Fri 0900–2100 (vacations and Spring bank holiday –1700). Sat 0900–1700 (term only). Closed Maundy Thur– Easter Mon. Late Summer bank holiday and 23–7 Dec.
Admission: At librarian's discretion (written application).
Enquiries: By post and telephone.
Microreading: Microfilm.
Copying: Xerox.
Lending: To members, to non-members at librarian's discretion, and through inter-library loan.
Union Record: BUCOP, BUCLA.

115 *West India Committee Library*

18 Grosvenor Street, London W1X 0HP
Tel: 01–629 6353
Librarian: W. Redmond
The library has been collecting in the field since about 1900 and now has approximately 8,000 titles. Special features of the collection are the materials on slavery, history, and sugar in the British West Indies, and the material which is being inter- mittently added falls under these subject headings. Newspapers are received by sea mail from almost all parts of the Common- wealth Caribbean, including Guyana but excluding Belize

(British Honduras). They are acquired by exchange against the *West Indies Chronicle* and are retained for between six weeks and six months. The *Jamaica Gleaner* comes by air freight.

Classified subject catalogue. Dewey classification. Open access.

Hrs: Mon 0930–1230. Fri 1300–1730. Closed bank holidays.
Admission: Open to general public.
Enquiries: By post.
Lending: None.

116   *Westminster City Libraries*

Marylebone Library (administrative headquarters)
Marylebone Road, London NW1 5PS
Tel: 01–828 8070
Telex: 263305 MARYLIB LDN

Central Reference Library (fine arts collection)
St Martin's Street, London WC2H 7HP
Tel: 01–930 3274
Telex: 261845 WESTMINLIB LDN

District Library (South Audley Street) (foreign languages collection)
20 South Audley Street, London W1Y 5DJ
Tel: 01–499 2351

Queen's Park Library,
666 Harrow Road, London W10 4NE
Tel: 01–969 0543

Central Music Library
District Library
Buckingham Palace Road, London SW1
Tel: 01–730 8921

City Librarian: K. C. Harrison MBE, FLA

Although, like that of most public libraries, the stock is largely limited to currently used material, Westminster acquires practically all United Kingdom material of any importance, and an appreciable proportion of North American publications. Its foreign acquisitions are also greater than most other public libraries. Latin American holdings amount to 3,000 books, 7 periodical titles, 200 music scores and 100 records. Present policy emphasises Latin American art and music, and Hispanic language and literature (a responsibility under the Inner London Subject Specialisation scheme, most of the stock being held at the District Library in South Audley Street). There are also books on the West Indies and by West Indian authors and 6 periodical titles. Additions consist almost entirely of current material. The Central Reference Library is notable for its worldwide map collection (22,000 items) and its holdings of official publications of the United Kingdom and international organisations.

Author and classified subject catalogues (Central Reference Library: alphabetical subject). Dewey classification. Open access.

Hrs: (Marylebone and Queen's Park libraries) Mon–Fri 0930–2000. Sat 0930–1700.

(Central Reference) Mon–Sat 1000–2000.

(South Audley Street) Mon–Fri 0930–1930. Sat 0930–1600.

(Central Music) Mon–Fri 0930–2000. Sat 0930–1700.

All libraries closed bank holidays and the Sat before Easter Sun.

Admission: Open to general public.

Enquiries: By post, telephone and Telex.

Microreading: Microcard and microfilm.

Copying: Xerox.

Lending: To holders of any U.K. public library ticket, and through inter-library loan, except records (limited to holders of G.L.C. public library tickets) and material at Central Reference Library (not lent).

Union Record: BLLD, BUCOP, LASER.

PUBLICATIONS:

Leaflet on foreign language collection.

Westminster union catalogue of periodicals, 1970.

MAIDSTONE

117　*East Malling Research Station*

Joint Library of the East Malling Research Station and the Commonwealth Bureau of Horticulture and Plantation Crops

East Malling, Maidstone, Kent. ME19 BJ

Tel: West Malling 843833 extn 236 (STD code 0732)

Librarian: Miss C. A. H. Jolly BSC, DIPLIB

The Joint Library is devoted to temperate and tropical fruits, vegetables, ornamentals and perennial plantation crops. Its total stock is of the order of 15,000 books and bound periodicals, 75,000 pamphlets, 300 annual reports and 850 current periodicals, some of the pamphlet and periodical material being obtained on exchange. Although no deliberate acquisition policy has been followed in relation to the West Indies or Latin America, some of the library's holdings are of relevance to the study of the area.

　　Author, title, alphabetical subject and classified subject catalogues. UDC classification. Open access.

Hrs: Mon–Fri 0840–1700. Closed bank holidays.

Admission: At librarian's discretion (prior application).

Enquiries: By post and telephone.

Microreading: Microfilm for staff members only.

Copying: Xerox.

Lending: To staff members and through inter-library loan.

Union Record: BLLD, LASER, COLAESS.

MANCHESTER

118　*Victoria University of Manchester*

John Rylands University Library of Manchester

Oxford Road, Manchester M13 9PP

Tel: 061–273 3333

Telex: 668932 UNIVLIBRY MCHR

University Librarian and Director: F. W. Ratcliffe MA, PHD

Subject enquiries to: J. T. D. Hall (Assistant Librarian in charge of Latin American studies)

The library began actively collecting in the field in 1962, and now has 7,500 books and 20 periodical titles. The collection is strong in the history and literature of Latin America and the Caribbean, with special emphasis placed on Brazil.

Author and classified subject catalogues. Dewey classification. Open access.

Hrs: Mon–Fri 0900–2130 (vacations 0930–1730). Sat 0900–1300. (Restricted areas open later Sat and also Sun except Summer vacation.) Closed bank holidays.

Admission: At librarian's discretion.

Enquiries: By post and telephone.

Microreading: Microcard, microfiche and microfilm.

Copying: Xerox.

Lending: To members and through inter-library loan.

Union Record: BUCOP, BUCLA.

PUBLICATIONS:

Readers' guide.

NEWCASTLE UPON TYNE

119 *University of Newcastle upon Tyne Library*

Queen Victoria Road, Newcastle upon Tyne NE1 7RU

Tel: Newcastle upon Tyne 28511 (STD code 0632)

Telex: 53654 UNIVLIB NCLE

University Librarian and Keeper of the Pybus Collection: B. J. Enright MA, DPHIL

The library has no special collection of Latin American material although holdings have been built up for first and postgraduate degree courses in Latin American studies. These include about 1,000 literary works and almost the same amount of history.

Author and classified subject catalogues. Dewey classification. Open access.

Hrs: Mon–Fri 0900–2100 (vacation –1700). Sat 0900–1630 (vacations –1300). Closed bank holidays.

Admission: At library committee's discretion (annual fee).

Microreading: Microcard, microfiche and microfilm.
Copying: Xerox.
Lending: To members and through inter-library loan.
Union Record: BLLD, BUCOP, BUCLA, NRLS.
PUBLICATIONS:
Guide to the library.

NOTTINGHAM

120   *Nottingham Public Libraries*

Central Library, South Sherwood Street, Nottingham NG1 4DA
Tel: Nottingham 43591 (STD code 0602)
Telex: 37662 INFORMLIB NOTTM
Librarian: P. Sykes DMA, FLA

The library is the East Midlands regional store for history and travel literature, in English, relating to Latin America and the Caribbean. It has 900 books, dating from 1930 onwards.

Author and classified subject catalogues. Dewey classification. Open access.

Hrs: Mon–Fri 0900–2000. Sat 0900–1600. Closed bank holidays.
Admission: Open to general public.
Enquiries: By post, telephone and Telex.
Microreading: Microfiche and microfilm.
Copying: Xerox.
Lending: To registered readers and through inter-library loan.
Union Record: BLLD, BUCOP, EMRLS.

OXFORD

121   *Bodleian Library, University of Oxford*

Oxford OX1 3BG
Tel: Oxford 44675 (STD code 0865)
Telex: 83656 BODLEIAN OXFORD
Bodley's Librarian: R. Shackleton MA, DLITT, FBA, FSA
Subject enquiries to: C. R. Steele MA, DIPLIB, ALA (Assistant with responsibility for Latin American purchases, extn 252 and 260)

The Bodleian Library has been acquiring books published on

Latin America and the Caribbean since 1602. As a result it now has the best collection in Great Britain outside the British Museum. The number of volumes held on the area is in excess of 70,000, whilst periodicals, both current and dead, total over 900. The various copyright privileges dating from 1610 have enabled the library to receive nearly all books published in England on Latin America and the Caribbean since that time. Purchases were made in Spain in the seventeenth century, but donations brought in even more material. The Bodleian's collection of Mexican codices, which includes those now called Laud, Mendoza and Selden, were received in this way. The library's holding of Latin American 'incunabula' is good, dating from 1544 for Mexico, and 1585 for Peru. An outstanding purchase of more recent times was the acquisition in 1870 of a large collection of Mexican independence pamphlets, which once belonged to Professor Henry Ward Poole. Purchasing declined because of lack of funds in the first half of the twentieth century, but revived with the establishment of a Parry Centre at Oxford in 1965. Special emphasis has been placed on the acquisition of material, both current and retrospective, in the humanities and social sciences covering the Andean republics, Argentina, Brazil and Mexico. Exchange agreements have been established with institutions and libraries in almost every Latin American country. The Map Section of the Bodleian has a large collection of maps on Latin America and the Caribbean, both historical and contemporary. See also Radcliffe Science Library (no. 129) and Rhodes House Library (no. 130).

Author catalogue. Own classification. Closed access.

Hrs: Mon–Fri 0900–2200 (vacations –1700 or –1900). Sat 0900–1900 (vacations –1300). Closed Good Fri–Easter Mon, first Wed after end of Trinity (Summer) term, week including Late Summer bank holiday, 24–31 Dec.

Admission: Bona fide researchers at librarian's discretion (written recommendation).

Enquiries: By post and telephone.

Microreading: Microcard, microfiche and microfilm.

Copying: Microfilm and Xerox.

Typewriters: Permitted.

Lending: Through inter-library loan.

Union Record: BUCOP, BUCLA, COLAESS, St Antony's College union catalogue of Latin Americana.

PUBLICATIONS:

Readers' guide.

C. R. Steele (ed.), *Periodicals relating to Latin American studies in the Bodleian Library, Oxford* (and 3 supplements).

C. R. Steele and M. P. Costeloe (eds), *Independent Mexico. A collection of Mexican pamphlets in the Bodleian Library*, London, Mansell, 1973.

A. R. Bonner, Mexican pamphlets in the Bodleian Library, *Bodleian Library Record* 8 (4), pp. 205–13.

A. R. Pagden (ed.), *Mexican pictorial manuscripts (Bodleian Library special picture books no. 4).*

122 *Department of Ethnology and Prehistory, University of Oxford*

Balfour Library

Pitt Rivers Museum, Parks Road, Oxford OX1 3PP

Tel: Oxford 54979 (STD code 0865)

Librarian: H. P. G. Unsworth

The library which was founded in 1940, collects material on the ethnology and prehistory of Latin America and the Caribbean, and has 400 books and 10 periodical titles.

Author and area catalogues. Own classification. Open access.

Hrs: Mon–Fri 0900–1230, 1400–1700 (vacations –1600). Closed Good Fri, 5 working days at Easter, 25–6 Dec and 5 working days at Christmas.

Admission: At librarian's discretion.

Enquiries: By post and telephone to members only.

Copying: Xerox.

Lending: To members.

Union Record: Union list of serials in the science area, Oxford.

123 *Department of Forestry, University of Oxford*

Forestry Library

Commonwealth Forestry Institute, South Parks Road, Oxford OX1 3RB

Tel: Oxford 57891 extn 5 (STD code 0865)
Librarian: E. F. Hemmings

The library, which was founded in 1908 and shares the Commonwealth Forestry Institute building with the Commonwealth Forestry Bureau, aims at worldwide acquisition of publications in forestry and related subjects, and has one of the largest collections in Great Britain. It began collecting material on Latin America and the Caribbean in the early twentieth century, and exchange arrangements have now been established with institutions in most Latin American countries.

Author, geographical and classified subject catalogues. Own classification (partly based on UDC). Open access.

Hrs: Mon–Fri 0900–1900 (vacations 0900–1300, 1415–1700). Sat 0900–1200 (term only). Closed bank holidays.
Admission: At librarian's discretion.
Enquiries: By post and telephone.
Microreading: Microcard, microfiche and microfilm.
Copying: Microfilm and Xerox.
Lending: Through inter-library loan.
Union Record: BLLD, BUCOP, SWRLS, COLAESS.
PUBLICATIONS:
List of periodicals and serials in the Forestry Library, 3rd edn, 1968.

124   *Institute of Agriculture Economics Library, University of Oxford*

Dartington House, Little Clarendon Street, Oxford OX1 2HP
Tel: Oxford 52921 extn 29 and 30 (STD code 0865)
Librarian: Miss S. F. Brown, ALA

The Institute library began collecting material on Latin America and the Caribbean in 1966 and specialises in acquiring books on agricultural economics and rural sociology. 10 periodical titles are taken and there is a standing order for reports of the Interamerican Committee for Agricultural Development.

Author and alphabetical subject catalogues. Own classification. Open access.

Hrs: Mon–Fri 0900–1800 (vacations 0900–1300, 1400–1730). Sat 0900–1230 (term only). Closed bank holidays.

Admission: At librarian's discretion (written recommendation).
Enquiries: By post and telephone.
Lending: To members and through inter-library loan.
Union Record: BUCOP, BUCLA, COLAESS, St Antony's College union catalogue of Latin Americana, *Union list of serials in the science area, Oxford.*

125 *Institute of Commonwealth Studies Library, University of Oxford*

Queen Elizabeth House, 21 St Giles, Oxford OX1 3LA
Tel: Oxford 52952 extn 24 (STD code 0865)
Librarian: R. J. Townsend

The library has been collecting on the Caribbean area since 1947 and has 375 volumes, 45 periodical titles and 560 pamphlets relating to current developments of a political, economic or social character in the area.

Author and (for the pamphlets only) alphabetical regional catalogue. Own classification. Open access.

Hrs: Mon–Fri 0900–1245, 1400–1900 (vacations –1700). Sat 0900–1245 (term only). Closed bank holidays (except Spring), seven working days at Easter and ten working days at Christmas.
Admission: Open to general public.
Enquiries: By post and telephone.
Copying: Xerox.
Lending: To users and through inter-library loan.
Union Record: COLAESS.
PUBLICATIONS:
Quarterly list of accessions 1950–.

126 *Institute of Economics and Statistics Library, University of Oxford*

St Cross Building, Manor Road, Oxford OX1 3UL
Tel: Oxford 49631 (STD code 0865)
Librarian: J. G. Watson MA

The library has an extensive collection of economic and statistical material published since 1945 on Latin America and the

Caribbean. Over 100 periodical titles are taken and blanket orders include those for RAND publications.

Author and classified subject catalogues. LC classification. Open access.

Hrs: Mon–Fri 0930–2200 (vacations –1800). Sat 0930–1300. Closed bank holidays, one week at Easter, the week including the Late Summer bank holiday and one week at Christmas.

Admission: At librarian's discretion.

Enquiries: By post and telephone.

Microreading: Microcard, microfiche and microfilm.

Copying: Xerox.

Lending: Through inter-library loan.

Union Record: BUCOP, BUCLA, COLAESS, St Antony's College union catalogue of Latin Americana.

PUBLICATIONS:

Latin American economic and social serials in the Institute of Economics and Statistics, 1968.

127   *Modern Languages Faculty Library (Spanish and Portuguese Section), University of Oxford*

65 St Giles, Oxford

Tel: Oxford 52739 (STD code 0865)

Assistant in charge of the Spanish and Portuguese Section: A. Seldon

The library is primarily intended for undergraduate reading, but also contains material intended for graduate readers. It is adjacent to the library of the Taylor Institution (no. 133). It has some 2,000 volumes and 3 periodicals on the literature of Latin America, and is specially strong on the Latin American novel. The library also has a fair holding of works relating to Brazilian literature.

Author catalogue. Own classification. Open access.

Hrs: Mon–Fri 1000–1300, 1430–1730. Sat 0900–1200. Closed vacations except first and last weeks.

Admission: At the discretion of the King Alfonso XIII Professor of Spanish Studies.

Microreading: Microcard.

Copying: Xerox.

Lending: To members.

Union Record: BUCLA, St Antony's College union catalogue of Latin Americana.

128 *Oxford Polytechnic Library*

Headington, Oxford ox3 obp
Tel: Oxford 63434 extn 15 and 49 (std code 0865)
Librarian: D. L. Smith ma, fla

Formerly the Oxford College of Technology, the Polytechnic began collecting material on Latin America and the Caribbean in 1958 and has a small collection of 200 volumes, including material on art and architecture.

Author and classified subject catalogues. Dewey classification. Open access.

Hrs: Mon–Fri 0900–2200 (vacation –1700). Sat 0900–1300 (term only).
Admission: Open to general public.
Enquiries: By post and telephone.
Microreading: Microfiche and microfilm.
Copying: Xerox.
Typewriters: Permitted.
Lending: To members, and through inter-library loan.
Union Record: SWRLS.
publications:
Readers' guide.

129 *Radcliffe Science Library, Bodleian Library, University of Oxford*

South Parks Road, Oxford ox1 3qp
Tel: Oxford 54161, Oxford 44675 (std code 0865)
Keeper of Scientific Books: D. H. Boalch ma

As the scientific section of the Bodleian Library, the library collects extensively in most scientific subjects, including mathematics, medicine and the history of science. Material of relevance to Latin America and the Caribbean includes naturalists' reports, and mining surveys. The actual scientific output of Latin America is not extensively collected.

Author catalogue. Own classification. Partly open access.

Hrs: Mon–Fri 0900–2200 (vacations –1700 or –1900). Sat 0900–1900 (vacations –1300). Closed as Bodleian Library.
Admission: As for Bodleian Library (no. 121).
Enquiries: By post and telephone.
Microreading: Microcard, microfiche and microfilm.
Copying: Xerox.
Lending: To senior members of the University and through inter-library loan.
Union Record: As for Bodleian (no. 121). Also *Union list of serials in the science area, Oxford.*
PUBLICATIONS:
Readers' guide.
Union list of serials in the science area, Oxford.

130   Rhodes House Library, University of Oxford

South Parks Road, Oxford OX1 3RG
Tel: Oxford 55762 (STD code 0865)
Librarian: F. E. Leese

Rhodes House Library is the section of the Bodleian Library devoted to the history and social sciences of the British colonies and Commonwealth (exclusive of Bangladesh, Pakistan, India and Burma), the United States and Africa (excluding the countries of the Mediterranean littoral but including the off-shore islands). As part of the Bodleian, the library holds the books on the above areas received under the Copyright Act. The library is particularly strong in the government publications of the British Caribbean and books and periodicals covering United States' relations with Latin America.

Author and classified subject catalogues. Own classification. Closed access.

Hrs: Mon–Fri 0900–1900 (vacations –1700). Sat 0900–1300. Closed as Bodleian Library.
Admission: Bona fide researchers (written recommendation).
Enquiries: By post and telephone.
Microreading: Microcard, microfiche and microfilm.
Copying: Microfilm and Xerox.
Lending: To members (from American and Commonwealth Lending Libraries) and through inter-library loan.

Union Record: BUCOP, COLAESS.

PUBLICATIONS:

Readers' Guide.

L. B. Frewer (ed.), *Manuscript collections (excluding Africana) in Rhodes House Library*, Oxford, 1970.

131 *Saint Antony's College, University of Oxford*

Latin American Centre Library

21 Winchester Road, Oxford OX2 6NA

Tel: Oxford 59651 extn 29 (STD code 0865)

College Librarian: Miss A. Abley ALA (St Antony's College Library, Woodstock Road, Oxford OX2 6JF)

Saint Antony's College is a research institution specialising in the history and politics of the modern world on a regional basis. Material on Latin America and the Caribbean is housed in the library of the Latin American Centre, which was established at the College in 1964 with the aid of a Ford Foundation Grant, and is under the supervision of M. D. Deas of the academic staff of the Centre. In 1965, Oxford University was invited to establish a Parry Centre, and the Latin American Centre became the focal point for Latin American studies in the University. The Centre houses a working library of 2,500 volumes, and a selection of periodicals, news reviews and newspapers. A special feature of the library is its extensive boxed collection of press cuttings and offprints. The Centre houses the Oxford Union Catalogue of Latin Americana.

Author and alphabetical subject catalogues. LC classification. Open access.

Hrs: Term: Mon–Fri 0930–1300, 1430–1730. Vacation hours vary.

Admission: On the introduction of a College Fellow or at the discretion of the College Librarian or the Secretary of the Centre (written application).

Enquiries: By post and telephone.

Microreading: Microfiche and microfilm.

Copying: Xerox.

Typewriters: Permitted.

Lending: To users, and through inter-library loan.

Union Record: BUCOP, BUCLA, St Antony's College union
catalogue of Latin Americana.

132 *School of Geography Library, University of Oxford*

Mansfield Road, Oxford OX1 3TB
Tel: Oxford 46134 (STD code 0865)
Librarian: Miss E. M. Buxton MA, FLA
The library has been collecting on Latin America and the
Caribbean since it was founded in 1889, and has 1270 government publications, 969 maps, 550 books, 300 pamphlets, 43
wall maps, and 3 periodical titles in the field. The collection is a
growing one, material from the Andean countries being
particularly well represented. The library also has a world wide
collection of meteorological records.

Author, alphabetical subject and classified subject catalogues.
Own classification. Open access.

Hrs: Mon–Fri 0900–1300, 1415–1900 (vacations 0900–1300,
1430–1700). Sat 0900–1300 (term only). Closed bank holi-
days (except Spring), one week at Christmas and one week
at Easter.
Admission: At librarian's discretion (recommendation preferred).
Enquiries: By post and telephone.
Microreading: Microcard, microfiche and microfilm.
Lending: To members, and through inter-library loan.
Union Record: BUCOP, BUCLA, COLAESS, St Antony's
College union catalogue of Latin Americana.
PUBLICATIONS:
Readers' guide.

133 *Taylor Institution Library, University of Oxford*

St Giles, Oxford OX1 3NA
Tel: Oxford 55059 (librarian), Oxford 57917 (library) (STD
code 0865)
Librarian: G. G. Barber BLITT, MA
Subject enquiries to: J. Wainwright BLITT, MA (Assistant with
responsibility for the Latin American section, Oxford 57917)
The Taylor Institution library, founded in 1845, complements

the Bodleian in that it is the university's main collection in the field of modern and medieval European languages and literatures. The library has an overall collection of about 250,000 volumes, into which the Latin American holdings, consisting of about 5,000 books and 20 periodicals are fully integrated. It is especially strong in its holdings of Argentine and Mexican literature. In addition to the works of Latin American writers, and critical works about them, the library also collects some essential historical, cultural and bibliographical background material. The bulk of the material on Latin America and the Caribbean has been acquired since 1965.

Author catalogue. Own classification. Closed access.

Hrs: Mon–Fri 0930–2200 (vacations 1000–1300, 1400–1700). Sat 0930–1300 (vacations 1000–1300). Closed Good Fri–Easter Mon, the week including the Late Summer bank holiday, the first Mon and Tues after the first Sun after 1 Sept, and one week at Christmas.

Admission: Bona fide graduate researchers.

Enquiries: By post and telephone.

Microreading: Microfiche and microfilm.

Copying: Microfilm and Xerox.

Lending: To readers.

Union Record: BUCLA, St Antony's College union catalogue of Latin Americana.

PUBLICATIONS:

Readers' guide.

PORTSMOUTH

134   *Portsmouth Polytechnic Library*

Hampshire Terrace, Portsmouth, Hants. POI 2EG

Tel: Portsmouth 27681 (STD code 0705)

Librarian: W. G. Gale BA, ALA

Subject enquiries to: R. R. Macdonald BA, DIPLIB, ALA (Humanities Library, D Block. Portsmouth 29912)

The library has been collecting in the field since 1969 and has 1,700 books and 37 periodicals. At present, Mexico is the main country represented in the collection, emphasis being given to literature, economics, history, sociology, geography and politics. Brazil, Argentina, Chile and Venezuela are the additional countries being emphasised in the current acquisi-tions policy.

Author and classified subject catalogues. Dewey classification. Open access.

Hrs: Mon–Thur 0900–2200 (vacations –1700). Fri 0900–2100 (vacations –1700) Sat 0900–1730. Sun 1400–1800. Closed bank holidays.

Admission: At librarian's discretion.

Enquiries: By post and telephone, to members only.

Microreading: Microcard, microfiche and microfilm.

Copying: Xerox.

Lending: To members, and through inter-library loan.

Union Record: BLLD, BUCLA.

PUBLICATIONS:

Guide to services.

Periodicals catalogue.

Guide to reference sources – Spanish/Latin American studies.

Weekly classified accessions list.

READING

135   *University of Reading Library*

The University, Whiteknights, Reading, Berks. RE6 2AE

Tel: Reading 84331 (STD code 0737)

University Librarian: J. Thompson, BA, FLA

The library, founded in 1893, has a small collection on Latin America and the Caribbean totalling 500 books and 20 periodicals.

Author and alphabetical subject catalogues. Dewey classifi-cation. Open access.

Hrs: Mon–Fri 0900–2215 (vacation –1700). Sat 0900–1800 (vacation –1230). Sun 1400–1800 (term only). Bank holiday hours vary.

Admission: Open to general public (prior application).

Enquiries: By post and telephone.

Microreading: Microcard, microfiche and microfilm.

Copying: Microfilm and Xerox.
Lending: To members and through inter-library loan.
Union Record: BLLD, BUCOP, BUCLA, LASER, COLAESS.
PUBLICATIONS:
Reading University Library handbook.

SAINT ANDREWS

136   *University of Saint Andrews Library*

South Street, Saint Andrews, Fife, Scotland. KY16 9TR
Tel: Saint Andrews 4333 (STD code 033 481)
Telex: 76213 UNIVLIB ST AND
Librarian: D. MacArthur MA, BSC, FLA

The library which benefited from copyright deposit provisions
between 1710 and 1836, now has 5,000 volumes and thirty
periodicals on Latin America and the Caribbean, current
emphasis being placed on the acquisition of economic and
linguistic studies and Brazilian literature. In building a collection of research materials for the study of Amerindian languages
and cultures, the library cooperates with the University of
Saint Andrews Centre for Latin American Linguistic Studies.

Author and classified subject catalogues. LC classification.
Closed access (except for certain categories of reader).

Hrs: Mon–Fri 0900–2200 (Summer vacation –1600, other
vacations –1700). Sat 0900–1215 (except Summer vacation).
Closed 1–2 Jan, 2nd Wed in August, 25 Dec.

Admission: Bonafide researchers (prior application; fee may be
required).

Enquiries: By post, and (to members only) by telephone.

Microreading: Microcard, microfiche and microfilm.

Copying: Microfilm and Xerox.

Typewriters: Permitted.

Lending: To members and through inter-library loan.

Union Record: BLLD, BUCOP, BUCLA, SCL, COLAESS.

PUBLICATIONS:

Readers' guide.

SALFORD

137   *University of Salford Library*

Salford, Lancs. M5 4WT
Tel: 061–736 5843 extn 7209
Telex: 668680 UNIV SALFORD
Librarian: A. C. Bubb BA, FLA

The library's major interests are science and technology, but its Latin American and Caribbean holdings, acquired since 1960, are principally in the fields of economics, geography, government, modern languages and sociology, and constitute only a small collection.

Author, title and classified subject catalogues. UDC classification. Open access.

Hrs: Mon–Fri 0900–2100 (vacation –1700). Sat 0900–1200 (term only). Closed bank holidays.
Admission: At librarian's discretion.
Enquiries: By post and telephone.
Microreading: Microcard, microfiche and microfilm.
Copying: Xerox.
Lending: To members and through inter-library loan.
Union Record: BLLD, BUCOP, BUCLA.
PUBLICATIONS:
Readers' guide.

SHEFFIELD

138   *Geographical Association*

Fleure Library
343 Fulwood Road, Sheffield, Yorks. S10 3BP
Tel: Sheffield 661666 (STD code 0742)
Librarian: Miss H. Todd BA, ALA

The library has about 400 books and pamphlets and 7 periodicals on the geography of Latin America.

Author and classified subject catalogues. Association of American Geographers' classification (modified). Open access.

Hrs: Mon, Thur–Fri 0900–1700, Tues–Wed 0900–1730. Closed bank holidays.

Admission: Open to general public.
Enquiries: By post and telephone.
Lending: To members.
PUBLICATIONS:
The Americas (library catalogue), 1968.

139   *University of Sheffield Library*

Western Bank, Sheffield, Yorks. s10 2TN
Tel: Sheffield 78555 (STD code 0742)
Telex: 54348 UNILIB SHEFFLD
Librarian: C. K. Balmforth MA, FLA

The library has about 2,500 books on Latin America predominantly in the literary field and holds 12 periodical titles.
From 1965 to 1967 the Library was one of two British members
of the Latin American Cooperative Acquisitions Project through
which it acquired material on economics, history, geography,
archaeology and literature.

Author and alphabetical subject catalogues. Dewey classification. Open access.

Hrs: Mon–Fri 0900–2130 (Summer term –2200, Summer and
Christmas vacations –1700). Sat 0900–1300 (in vacation
–1230). Sun 1400–1800 during first 5 weeks of the Summer
term only. Closed bank holidays (except Spring bank holiday
0900–1700).
Admission: At librarian's discretion.
Enquiries: By post and telephone.
Microreading: Microcard, microfiche and microfilm.
Copying: Microfilm and Xerox.
Lending: To members and through inter-library loan.
Union Record: BLLD (foreign material only), BUCOP, BUCLA,
COLAESS.
PUBLICATIONS:
Readers' guide to the library.
Various bibliographies and subject guides.

SOUTHAMPTON

140   *University of Southampton Library*

Highfield, Southampton, Hants. so9 5NH
Tel: Southampton 559122 (STD code 0703)
Telex: 47661 UNIV SOTON
University Librarian: B. M. Bland MCOM
The library's collection on Latin America is intended to support
the university's teaching programmes in politics, history and
literature and consists of about 2,500 volumes and about 10
current serials.
  Author and classified subject catalogues. LC classification.
Open access.
Hrs: Mon–Fri 0900–2200. Sat 0900–1700. Sun 1400–1800.
  Closed bank holidays (except Spring) and 2 days in July.
Admission: At librarian's discretion (written recommendation
  or other identification).
Enquiries: By post and telephone.
Microreading: Microcard, microfiche and microfilm.
Copying: Microfilm and Xcrox.
Lending: To members, other registered borrowers (fee required),
  and through inter-library loan.
Union Record: BLLD, BUCOP, SWRLS, COLAESS.
PUBLICATIONS:
Introducing the library.

SOUTHEND-ON-SEA

141   *Southend-on-Sea Public Libraries*

Central Library
Victoria Avenue, Southend-on-Sea, Essex. ss2 6EX
Tel: Southend-on-Sea 49451 extn 539 (STD code 0702)
Librarian: L. Helliwell FLA

A scheme of cooperative book selection begun by the former
South Eastern Regional Library Bureau (SERLB) in 1955 gave
Southend Public Library the responsibility of acquiring all

publications appearing in the *British National Bibliography* under Dewey classes 918 and 980 (South American travel and history), together with certain fields of South American economic history, with the option of excluding books above a stated price level. When the SERLB was merged with the corresponding County of London cooperative organisation (LUC) in 1969, to form the London and South Eastern (Library) Region, (LASER), this subject responsibility passed to Hackney Public Library (no. 87), but Southend Public Library decided to continue purchasing in this area to much the same extent as before. Hitherto Southend automatically received other libraries' stock withdrawals within the speciality; now, however, first refusal of such material is offered to Hackney. The library now has over 1,300 titles in the field.

Author, title and alphabetical subject catalogues. Dewey classification. Open access.

Hrs: Mon–Tues, Thur–Fri 0930–1900. Wed 0930–1700. Sat 0900–1700. Closed bank holidays.

Admission: Open to general public.

Enquiries: By post and telephone.

Microreading: Microfilm.

Copying: Xerox.

Lending: To users (readers' tickets from other U.K. public libraries accepted), and through inter-library loan.

Union Record: BLLD, LASER.

STIRLING

142   *University of Stirling Library*

Stirling, Scotland. FK9 4LA

Tel: Stirling 3171 extn 2226/7 (STD code 0786)

Telex: 778874 UNILIB STERLING

Librarian: P. G. Peacock BA

Subject enquiries to: R. J. Davis BA, DIPLIB (Sub-Librarian, Chief Cataloguer, extn 2236)

The library began collecting material on Latin America and the Caribbean in 1966 and now has 450 volumes and 6 periodicals, principally in the fields of history and sociology.

Author, alphabetical subject and classified subject catalogues. Own classification. Open access.

Hrs: Mon–Fri 0900–2200 (vacations –1700). Sat 0900–1230 (term only). Sun 1400–1700 (term only). Closed Scottish bank holidays, 2 Jan, Good Fri to Easter Mon, one day in mid Aug, one day in late Oct/early Nov.

Admission: Open to general public.

Enquiries: By post and telephone.

Microreading: Microcard, microfiche and microfilm.

Copying: Xerox.

Typewriters: Permitted.

Lending: To members and through inter-library loan.

Union Record: BUCLA.

PUBLICATIONS:

Readers' guide.

SURBITON

143 *Directorate of Overseas Surveys, Technical Services Division, Overseas Development Administration, Foreign and Commonwealth Office*

Kingston Road, Tolworth, Surbiton, Surrey. KT5 9NS

Tel: 01–337 8661

Librarians: (Book library) A. J. Gillies BSC (extn 35)
(Map library) Miss E. V. Saunders BSC (extn 41)
(Air-photo library) Mrs M. C. M. O'Brien BSC (extn 43)
(Survey data library) R. T. Porter BA (extn 42)

The Directorate, set up in 1946, is concerned with the production of maps of many Commonwealth countries, including all the former British West Indies, Belize, Guyana, Bermuda and the Falkland Islands. The Technical Services Division collects all types of material required for map production. It consists of a *Map Library* which aims to include all maps containing topographical information about the countries of interest to the Directorate, a *Survey data library*, containing the original records of the Directorate's field surveyors, an *Air-photo library*, including original negatives, and a *Book library* of about 13,000

books and pamphlets and 500 current serial titles, which specialises in geodesy, land survey, cartography, photogrammetry,
land and survey legislation, and has some coverage of land
tenure and other aspects of the social and economic background
of the countries concerned, and data on international bound-
aries. In addition to West Indian material, the book library
also holds a limited amount of material on mapping and air
photo cover in the other countries of Latin America.

Author and classified subject catalogues. UDC classification.
Open access.

Hrs: Mon–Fri 0900–1630. Closed bank holidays and Fri before
Spring bank holiday.

Admission: Bona fide researchers (prior notice).

Enquiries: By post and telephone.

Copying: Xerox.

Lending: To members and (occasionally) to non-members and
through inter-library loan.

144 *Land Resources Division Library, Overseas Development
Administration, Foreign and Commonwealth Office*

Tolworth Tower, Surbiton, Surrey. KT6 7DY
Tel: 01–399 5281 extn 342
Librarian: N. W. Posnett BSC, AIINFSC

The library began collecting material on land resource assessment in Latin America and the West Indies in 1964.

Author catalogue. UDC classification. Open access.

Hrs: Mon–Fri 0900–1630. Closed bank holidays.

Admission: At librarian's discretion (prior application requested).

Enquiries: By post.

Microreading: Microcard, microfiche and microfilm.

Copying: Xerox.

Lending: To members and (exceptionally) to non-members,
and through inter-library loan.

SWANSEA

145   *University College of Swansea Library, University of Wales*

Singleton Park, Swansea, Wales. SA2 8PP
Tel: Swansea 25678 extn 272 (STD code 0792)
Telex: 48358 UNIVLIB SWANSEA
Librarian: F. J. W. Harding BLITT, MA, ALA, FLS, FRHISTS, FSA
The library began collecting material on Latin America and the West Indies in 1955 and currently has 420 volumes and 14 periodical titles.
    Author and alphabetical subject catalogues. LC classification. Open access.
Hrs: Mon–Fri 0900–2200 (vacation –1700). Sat 0900–1700 (vacation –1200). Sun 1400–1800 (term only). Closed bank holidays (except Spring), one week at Easter and one week at Christmas.
Admission: At librarian's discretion (written application).
Enquiries: By post and telephone.
Microreading: Microcard, microfiche and microfilm.
Copying: Microfilm and Xerox.
Typewriters: Permitted.
Lending: To members and through inter-library loan.
Union Record: BLLD, BUCOP, WRLS.
PUBLICATIONS:
Union list of current periodicals in the University of Wales, 1972.

UXBRIDGE

146   *Brunel University Library*

Kingston Lane, Uxbridge, Middx. UB8 3PH
Tel: Uxbridge 37188 (STD code 0895; London area local code 89)
University Librarian: C. N. Childs BA
The library's general collection contains a very small number of books on Latin America, collected during the last five years, which are shelved with the rest of the collection.

Author, title and alphabetical subject catalogues. LC classification. Open access.

Hrs: Mon–Thur 0900–2100 (vacations 0930–1700). Fri 0900–
1900 (vacations 0930–1700). Sat 0930–1230. Closed bank
holidays, one week at Easter and one week at Christmas.

Admission: At librarian's discretion.

Enquiries: By post and telephone.

Microreading: Microcard, microfiche and microfilm.

Copying: Xerox.

Lending: To members, and through inter-library loan.

Union Record: BLLD.

PUBLICATIONS:

Guide to the library.

Serials list.

APPENDIX

OTHER SOURCES OF INFORMATION

This section begins with a list of certain bodies which are actively concerned with more than one country in the area, and continues with a section devoted to each individual country. No attempt has been made to include consular offices outside London. The appendix also contains a list of other British groups concerned with Latin America, and a list of relevant serial publications.

BODIES CONCERNED WITH MORE THAN ONE COUNTRY

British Council: 65 Davies Street, London w1. *Tel:* 01–499 8011.

Commonwealth Secretariat: Marlborough House, Pall Mall, London sw1y 5hx. *Tel:* 01–839 3411. See also entry number 64.

Foreign and Commonwealth Office: Downing Street, London sw1. *Tel:* 01–930 8440. See also entry numbers 70, 143 and 144.

International Coffee Organization: 22 Berners Street, London w1p 4dd. *Tel:* 01–580 8591. See also entry number 83.

International Sugar Organization: 28 Haymarket, London sw1y 4sp. *Tel:* 01–930 3666.

International Tin Council: 28 Haymarket, London sw1y 4sp. *Tel:* 01–930 0321.

International Wheat Council: 28 Haymarket, London sw1y 4sp. *Tel:* 01–930 4128.

BODIES CONCERNED WITH ONE
COUNTRY

ANTIGUA

The diplomatic representation of Antigua is the responsibility
of the British Foreign Office.

National Tourist Agency: Antigua Tourist Office, 200 Buckingham Palace Road, London SW1. *Tel:* 01–730 6221.

ARGENTINA

Embassy (and departments not listed below): 9 Wilton Crescent, London SW1X 8RP. *Tel:* 01–235 3717.

Air and Military Attachés: 6 Tilney Street, London W1Y 5LD. *Tel:* 01–499 8138.

Economic and Financial Sections: 111 Cadogan Gardens, London SW3 2RQ. *Tel:* 01–730 4388.

General Consulate: 53 Hans Place, London SW1. *Tel:* 01–584 1701.

Naval Attaché: 242 Vauxhall Bridge Road, London SW1V 1AU. *Tel:* 01–834 2802.

Airline Office: Aerolíneas Argentinas, 18 New Bond Street, London W1. *Tel:* 01–493 6941.

National Bank: Banco de la Nación Argentina, 2nd Floor, Goodenough House, 33 Old Broad Street, London EC2. *Tel:* 01–283 8989 extn 3284.

Anglo-Argentine Society: 2 Belgrave Square, London SW1. *Tel:* 01–235 9505.

BAHAMAS

High Commissioner (and all departments): 39 Pall Mall, London SW1. *Tel:* 01–930 6967.

Airline Office: Air Bahama, 45 South Audley Street, London W1. *Tel:* 01–629 7944 and 01–499 6721.

BARBADOS

High Commissioner (and all departments): 6 Upper Belgrave Street, London SW1X 8AZ. *Tel:* 01–235 8686/9.

Airline Office: International Caribbean Airways, 9–13 Grosvenor Street, London W1X 0EE. *Tel:* 01–492 1157.

National Tourist Agency: Barbados Board of Tourism, 6 Upper Belgrave Street, London sw1x 8az. *Tel:* 01-235 2449.

BELIZE
An internally self-governing British colony, known until June 1973 as British Honduras, whose diplomatic representation is the responsibility of the British Foreign Office.

BERMUDA
An internally self-governing British colony, whose diplomatic representation is the responsibility of the British Foreign Office.
National Bank: Bank of Bermuda, 35 Bishopsgate, London ec2. *Tel:* 01-600 0606.
National Tourist Agency: Bermuda Department of Tourism, 58 Grosvenor Street, London w1x 0jd. *Tel:* 01-499 1777.

BOLIVIA
Embassy (and departments not listed below): 106 Eaton Square, London sw1w 9ad. *Tel:* 01-235 4248.
Consulate: 106 Eccleston Mews, London sw1. *Tel:* 01-235 4255.

BRAZIL
Embassy (and departments not listed below): 32 Green Street, London w1y 4at. *Tel:* 01-629 0155. *Telex:* 261157. See also entry number 49.
Commercial Section: Brazilian Trade Centre, 15 Berkeley Street, London w1x 5ae. *Tel:* 01-499 6706-8.
General Consulate: 6 Deanery Street, London w1y 5lh. *Tel:* 01-499 7441.
Airline Office: VARIG Brazilian Airlines, 235 Regent Street, London w1.
Brazilian Chamber of Commerce and Economic Affairs in Great Britain: 35 Dover Street, London w1. *Tel:* 01-499 0186.
National Banks: Banco do Brasil, 60/63 Aldermanbury, London ec2v 7jy. *Tel:* 01-600 8981. Banco do Estado de São Paulo, Plantation House, 31/35 Fenchurch Street, London ec3m 3na. *Tel:* 01-623 2291.
Anglo-Brazilian Society: 2 Belgrave Square, London sw1. *Tel:* 01-235 3751.

Casa do Brasil (House of Brazil): 49 Lancaster Gate, London w2. *Tel:* 01–723 9648.

PETROBRAS (Brazilian Oil Company Office): 3rd Floor, Berk House, 8 Baker Street, London w1. *Tel:* 01–935 3391.

EUROBRAS (European Brazilian Bank): St Helen's, Undershaft, London EC3. *Tel:* 01–623 8281.

BRITISH HONDURAS see BELIZE

BRITISH VIRGIN ISLANDS
A group of over 60 islands which together constitute a British territory and whose diplomatic representation is the responsibility of the British Foreign Office.

BRITISH WEST INDIES
The term British West Indies is used to cover the Cayman Islands, the Turks and Caicos Islands, relevant British possessions in the Leeward Islands (Antigua, Montserrat, and St Kitts, Nevis and Anguilla) and in the Windward Islands (Dominica, Grenada, St Lucia and St Vincent). The diplomatic representation of these territories is the responsibility of the British Foreign Office. The Bahamas, Barbados, Jamaica, and Trinidad and Tobago, which formerly were a part of this category are now independent countries and separately listed. Though not independent, Antigua is also separately listed.

British West Indian Airways Limited: 16 Maddox Street, London w1. *Tel:* 01–493 1242.

Eastern Caribbean Tourist Boards: 200 Buckingham Palace Road, London sw1. *Tel:* 01–730 6221.

CHILE
Embassy (and departments not listed below): 12 Devonshire Street, London win 2ds. *Tel:* 01–580 6392/4.

Air Attaché: 12 Devonshire Street, London win 2ds. *Tel:* 01–580 1691.

Commercial Counsellor: Copper Corporation, Bush House, 100/101 Aldwych, London wc2. *Tel:* 01–240 2191.

General Consulate: 12 Devonshire Street, London win 2ds. *Tel:* 01–580 1023.

Naval and Military Attaché: Chilean Naval Mission, Piccadilly House, 33 Regent Street, London SW1. *Tel:* 01–734 0802. *Telex:* 21449.
Anglo-Chilean Society: 12 Devonshire Street, London WIN 2DS. *Tel:* 01–580 1271. See also entry number 45.

COLOMBIA

Embassy (and departments not listed below): Flat 3, 3 Hans Crescent, London SW1X OLR. *Tel:* 01–589 9177.
Consulate General: 10 Park Lane, London W1. *Tel:* 01–493 4566.
Airline Office: AVIANCA, 170 Piccadilly, London W1. *Tel:* 01–759 2595.
Permanent Delegation to the International Coffee Organization: 140 Park Lane, London W1. *Tel:* 01–493 4565 and 193 Piccadilly, London W1. *Tel:* 01–734 4144.
Anglo-Colombian Society: 5 Belgrave Square, London SW1. *Tel:* 01–235 3601.

COSTA RICA

Embassy (and departments not listed below): 8 Braemar Mansions, Cornwall Gardens, London SW7 4AF. *Tel:* 01–937 7883.
Consulate: 8 Braemar Mansions, Cornwall Gardens, London SW7 4AF. *Tel:* 01–937 7749.

CUBA

Embassy (and departments not listed below): 57 Kensington Court, London W8 5DQ. *Tel:* 01–937 8226. *Telex:* 262148.
Commercial Section: 54 Conduit Street, London WIR OBY. *Tel:* 01–734 9031/40. *Telex:* 261094.
National Bank: Banco Nacional de Cuba, 104 Leadenhall Street, London EC3. *Tel:* 01–623 2707, (foreign exchange) 01–623 2244.

DOMINICAN REPUBLIC

Embassy (and departments not listed below): 4 Braemar Mansions, Cornwall Gardens, London SW7 4AG. *Tel:* 01–937 1921. *Telex:* 918817.
General Consulate: 4 Braemar Mansions, Cornwall Gardens, London SW7 4AG. *Tel:* 01–937 7116.

DUTCH GUIANA see SURINAM

ECUADOR

Embassy (and all departments): Flat 3B, 3 Hans Crescent, London SWIX OLS. *Tel:* 01–584 1367.

FRENCH GUIANA

An Overseas Department of France, whose diplomatic representation in overseas countries is carried out by the accredited representatives of France.

French Embassy: 58 Knightsbridge, London SWIX 7JT. *Tel:* 01–235 8080.

. FRENCH WEST INDIES

The French West Indies consist principally of Martinique and Guadeloupe, both of which form part of the Windward Islands, and are Overseas Departments of France. Their diplomatic representation in overseas countries is carried out by the accredited representatives of France.

French Embassy: 58 Knightsbridge, London SWIX 7JT. *Tel:* 01–235 8080.

GUATEMALA

Diplomatic relations between Britain and Guatemala are in suspense.

Airline Office: Aviateca Guatemala International Airlines, 14 Red Lion Square, London WC1. *Tel:* 01–405 5316.

GUYANA

High Commissioner (and all departments): 28 Cockspur Street, London SWIY 5DE. *Tel:* 01–930 1994/6. *Telex:* 916812. *Cable address:* Guycom, London.

HAITI

Embassy (and all departments): 17 Queen's Gate, London SW7 5JE. *Tel:* 01–581 0577.

HONDURAS

Embassy (and departments not listed below): 48 George Street, London WIH 5RF. *Tel:* 01–486 3380.

Consular Section: 48 George Street, London WIH 5RF. *Tel:* 01–486 4880.

JAMAICA

High Commissioner (and departments not listed below): 48 Grosvenor Street, London WIX 9FH. *Tel:* 01–499 8600.
Consular Section: 20–22 Mount Row, London WI. *Tel:* 01–499 8600.
National Bank: Jamaican Development Bank, 10 Storey Gate, London SWI. *Tel:* 01–839 1503.

MEXICO

Embassy (and departments not listed below): 8 Halkin Street, London SWIX 7DW. *Tel:* 01–235 6393/6. *Telex:* 918276.
Commercial Section: 52 Grosvenor Gardens, 8th Floor, London SWI. *Tel:* 01–730 6416.
Airline Office: AEROMEXICO, 6 Vigo Street, London WI. *Tel:* 01–437 0389.
National Bank: Banco de Comercio S.A., 80 Gracechurch Street, London EC3. *Tel:* 01–626 3511.
National Tourist Agency: Mexican National Tourist Office, 52 Grosvenor Gardens, London SWI. *Tel:* 01–730 0128.
British-Mexican Society: 52 Grosvenor Gardens, London SWI. *Tel:* 01–730 0128.

NETHERLANDS ANTILLES

The Netherlands Antilles consist of the five islands of Aruba, Bonaire, Curaçao, Saba and Sint Eustatius, and the southern part of the island of Sint Maarten (Saint Martin) the northern part of which is included in the French department of Guadeloupe (see French West Indies). All of these lie in the Lesser Antilles group, and form part of the Kingdom of the Netherlands. Their diplomatic representation in overseas countries is carried out by the Diplomatic and Consular corps of the Kingdom of the Netherlands.
Royal Netherlands Embassy: 38 Hyde Park Gate, London SW7 5DP. *Tel:* 01–584 5040.

NICARAGUA

Embassy (and all departments): 8 Gloucester Road, London sw7 4PP. *Tel:* 01–584 3231.

PANAMA

Embassy (and departments not listed below): 29 Wellington Court, 116 Knightsbridge, London sw1x 7PJ. *Tel:* 01–584 5540.
Consulate General: Wheatsheaf House, 4 Carmelite Street, London EC4Y OBN. *Tel:* 01–353 4792/3.

PARAGUAY

Embassy (and departments not listed below): Braemar Lodge, Cornwall Gardens, London sw7 4AQ. *Tel:* 01–937 1253.
Consular Section: Braemar Lodge, Cornwall Gardens, London sw7 4AQ. *Tel:* 01–937 6629.

PERU

Embassy (and departments not listed below): 52 Sloane Street, London sw1x 9SP. *Tel:* 01–235 1917 and 01–235 2545.
Air and Military Attaché: 52 Sloane Street, London sw1x 9SP. *Tel:* 01–235 9826.
Commercial Attaché: 52 Sloane Street, London sw1x 9SP. *Tel:* 01–235 8975.
Consular Section: 52 Sloane Street, London sw1x 9SP. *Tel:* 01–235 6867.
Naval Attaché: 52 Sloane Street, London sw1x 9SP. *Tel:* 01–235 8340.
Airline Office: APSA, Aereolíneas Peruanas S.A., 162 Regent Street, London w1. *Tel:* 01–437 1747.
Anglo-Peruvian Society: 52 Sloane Street, London sw1x 9SP. *Tel:* 01–235 3601.

PUERTO RICO

Puerto Rico is an Overseas Commonwealth Territory of the United States of America. Diplomatic representation in overseas countries is the responsibility of the State Department of the United States of America.

Embassy of the United States of America: Grosvenor Square, London WIA IAE. *Tel:* 01–499 9000.

EL SALVADOR

Embassy (and all departments): Flat 16, Edinburgh House, 9B Portland Place, London WIN 3AA. *Tel:* 01–636 9563/4. *Telex:* 236394.
National Tourist Agency Office: Flat 16, Edinburgh House, 9B Portland Place, London WIN 3AA.

SURINAM

A fully autonomous and equal partner in the Kingdom of the Netherlands, whose diplomatic representation in overseas countries is carried out by the Diplomatic and Consular Corps of the Kingdom of the Netherlands.

Royal Netherlands Embassy: 38 Hyde Park Gate, London SW7 5DP. *Tel:* 01–584 5040.

TRINIDAD AND TOBAGO

High Commissioner (and all departments): 42 Belgrave Square, London SW1X 8NT. *Tel:* 01–245 9351. *Telex:* 918910 TRINTAGOF LDN.
Airline Office: British West Indian Airways, 16 Maddox Street, London W1. *Tel:* 01–493 1242.

URUGUAY

Embassy (and departments not listed below): 48 Lennox Gardens, London SW1X ODL. *Tel:* 01–589 8835/6. *Telex:* 264180.
Consulate General: 48 Lennox Gardens, London SW1X ODL. *Tel:* 01–589 8735.
British-Uruguayan Society: Shreelane, 222 Brooklands Road, Weybridge, Surrey. *Tel:* Weybridge 47455 (STD code 0254 82; London local code 97).

VENEZUELA

Embassy (and departments not listed below): Flat 6, 3 Hans Crescent, London SW1X OLX. *Tel:* 584 4206/7. *Telex:* 264186. See also entry number 111.
Air Attaché: 82 Palace Court, London W2 4JF. *Tel:* 01–229 8230 and 1483.

Consulate General: 71A Park Mansions, 141/9 Knightsbridge, London SW1. *Tel:* 01–589 1121.
Military and Naval Attachés: 59 Palace Court, London W2 *Tel:* 01–229 8939.
Airline Office: VIASA, Venezuelan International Airways S.A., 65 Grosvenor Street, London W1. *Tel:* 01–629 1223.

VIRGIN ISLANDS OF THE UNITED STATES OF AMERICA

A group of 40 islands and cays, the largest of which are St Thomas, St John and St Croix, and which form an unincorporated territory of the United States. Diplomatic representation in overseas countries is the responsibility of the State Department of the United States of America.

Embassy of the United State of America: Grosvenor Square, London WIA IAE. *Tel:* 01–499 9000.

OTHER GROUPS CONCERNED WITH LATIN AMERICA

Committee on Latin America (COLA). Secretary: G. H. Green, Librarian, Hispanic and Luso-Brazilian Council, 2 Belgrave Square, London SW1X 8PJ. *Tel:* 01–235 2303/7.
Society for Latin American Studies. Secretary: R. F. Colson, Department of History, University of Southampton, Highfield, Southampton S09 5NM. *Tel:* Southampton 559122 (STD code 0703).
Standing Conference of National and University Libraries (SCONUL), Latin American Group. Secretary: B. Naylor, Secretary, ILRCC, University of London, Senate House, London WC1E 7HU. *Tel:* 01–636 4514.

JOURNALS AND SERIES

British Bulletin of Publications on Latin America, the West Indies, Portugal and Spain. The Hispanic and Luso-Brazilian Council, 2 Belgrave Square, London SW1X 8PJ. Twice a year.

Bulletin of Hispanic Studies. Liverpool University Press, 123 Grove Street, Liverpool L7 7AF. Quarterly.

Bulletin of the Society for Latin American Studies. c/o Department of History, University of Southampton, Highfield, Southampton SO9 5NM. Termly.

Journal of Latin American Studies. Cambridge University Press, Bentley House, 200 Euston Road, London NW1 2DB. Twice a year.

Latin America. Latin American Newsletters Limited, 69 Cannon Street, London EC4N 5AB. Weekly.

Latin America Review of Books. Latin America Review of Books Limited, 69 Cannon Street, London EC4N 5AB and 84 Woodhouse Lane, Leeds LS2 8AB. Irregular.

Latin American Monographs Series. Published by the Athlone Press for the Institute of Latin American Studies, University of London, 31 Tavistock Square, London WC1H 9HA. Irregular.

Latin American Studies in the Universities of the United Kingdom. Institute of Latin American Studies, University of London, 31 Tavistock Square, London WC1H 9HA. Annually.

Monograph Series. Centre for Latin-American Studies, University of Liverpool, 86/88 Bedford Street South, Liverpool L69 3BX. Irregular.

Occasional Papers. Institute of Latin-American Studies, University of Glasgow, 5 University Gardens, Glasgow G12 8QH. Irregular.

Occasional Papers. St Antony's College, Latin American Centre, 21 Winchester Road, Oxford OX2 6JF. Irregular.

Staff Research in Progress or Recently Completed in the Humanities and Social Sciences. Institute of Latin American Studies, University of London, 31 Tavistock Square, London WC1H 9HA. Annually.

Theses in Latin American Studies at British Universities in Progress and Completed. Institute of Latin American Studies, University of London, 31 Tavistock Square, London WC1H 9HA. Annually.

Working Papers. Centre of Latin American Studies, University of Cambridge, History Faculty Building, West Road, Cambridge CB3 9EF. Irregular.

INDEX

Note: The index covers libraries and named collections by title, acronym, locality, parent organisation and subject interest. Subject entries should be treated with reserve. For some newly initiated collections, subject interest may imply little more than a hopeful statement of intent. On the other hand since reference has normally been restricted to subjects (or their apparent synonyms) specifically mentioned in a library's entry, many excellent collections have doubtless been overlooked, particularly in the larger, general libraries. The index does not cover the contents of the appendix.

References in the index are to entry numbers

94006